# Judith Allen Shelly

# Not Just a Job

## Serving Christ in Your Work

D0039042

INTERVARSITY PRESS
DOWNERS GROVE, ILLINOIS 60515

*InterVarsity Press is the book-publishing division of Inter-Varsity Christian Fellowship, a student movement active on campus at hundreds of universities, colleges and schools of nursing. For information about local and regional activities, write IVCF, 233 Langdon St., Madison, WI 53703.*

*Distributed in Canada through InterVarsity Press, 860 Denison St., Unit 3, Markham, Ontario L3R 4H1, Canada.*

*Cover illustration: Greg Wray*

*All Scripture quotations, unless otherwise indicated, are from the Revised Standard Version of the Bible, copyrighted 1946, 1952,© 1971, 1973.*

*The information in the appendix is adapted from* Lifestyle of Love *by Mary Thompson,* © *1978 by Inter-Varsity Christian Fellowship of the United States of America. Used by permission of InterVarsity Press.*

*ISBN 0-87784-332-5*

*Printed in the United States of America*

Library of Congress Cataloging in Publication Data
*Shelly, Judith Allen.*
    *Not just a job.*

    *Bibliography: p.*
        *1. Work (Theology)   2. Christian life—1960-*
*I. Title.*
*BT738.5.S55       1985          248.4          84-29676*
*ISBN 0-87784-332-5*

| 18 | 17 | 16 | 15 | 14 | 13 | 12 | 11 | 10 | 9 | 8 | 7 | 6 | 5 | 4 | 3 | 2 | 1 |
| 99 | 98 | 97 | 96 | 95 | 94 | 93 | 92 | 91 | 90 | 89 | 88 | 87 | 86 | 85 | | | |

*To Janelle and Jonathan,*
*who radically changed and enriched*
*my work,*
*and to Jim, who has*
*loved, supported and encouraged me*
*through it all.*

# Introduction

Even in a leisure-oriented society work consumes most of our waking hours. Work on the job, housework, volunteer work vie for our time, attention and loyalty, along with the demands of family and friends and the need to rest periodically. We even work at our leisure. The coveted recreational vehicle has to be maintained. The child's swing set must be assembled. The beautiful lawn has to be mowed and the garden weeded. Suddenly everyone is talking about "burnout," and it is no wonder.

For the Christian, work is more than just a way to put food on the table and fill the time. It is a call from God. We work because God created us with gifts and talents to be used for his glory in the world. God intends for our work to be meaningful, purposeful, and even fun. However, all too often the pressures of day-to-day existence sap our sense of joy and fulfillment. Sometimes this happens when we do not seek the Lord's direction for our work. We may assume that he couldn't possibly want us to do something we enjoy—or we may feel that he wants us to say yes to every opportunity to serve. We end up either bored and frustrated or tense and exhausted.

This book is designed to provide a way out of the work dilemma. First it presents a theological basis for work as a call from God and shows how that applies to our daily lives. Next it provides guidelines for seeking God's will about our work. Finally it gives practical ways to balance the various dimensions of work and life.

There is no such thing as "just a job" for a Christian. We are called to serve Christ as priests and prophets in the world. No matter where we serve or what we do we are ministers of the gospel. Carefully planning the nature and direction of our work can make us more effective in that ministry. It is not just a one-time career choice, but a lifelong struggle to stay in the center of God's will and find balance in our lives. I hope this book will make that struggle a little bit easier.

# 1
# God's Call
# to Work

W HAT ARE YOU GOING to be when you grow up?"

You've heard that question since you were two. By the time you were four you knew the answer—you'd be a policeman like Dad or a lawyer like Mom. Then you started school and the world expanded. You realized that the options were greater. New dreams and self-images entered your thinking. For a while you wanted to be a ballerina, then a teacher or maybe a professional ball player or a pastor. But then, as high school drew to a close, you became more philosophical. The question got bigger and harder to answer.

"Why am I here?"

Most of us ask ourselves that question at least occasionally. Crisis periods—times when we must make major life-changing decisions—often precipitate deep soul-searching about our personal meaning and purpose in life. The jobs we seek or the career we strive for are only a part of the picture. We want our lives to count for something. But it doesn't take long to learn that idealism doesn't pay very well. Suddenly we are back to the old, practical question.

"What am I going to do for a living?"

During my junior year in high school I began to think seriously about what I wanted to do with my life. Suddenly it dawned on me that I was responsible for making decisions that would affect the way I lived the rest of my life. At the time, I believed those choices would be final and unchangeable. Being a practical person, I set out to research the options available to me. I made a list of all the things I liked to do and another list of all the jobs that somewhat intrigued me. Then I conducted formal interviews with people in the community, asking them about the positive and negative aspects of their chosen fields, the salary range, the educational preparation, and the opportunities for advancement. Finally, nursing, teaching and Christian education worked their way to the top of the list. My research continued as I tested each field by working as a hospital volunteer and as the school nurse's assistant, volunteering to teach a chemistry class on student-teacher day, serving as an assistant Girl Scout leader, teaching Sunday school, and appointing myself assistant to the director of Christian education at church.

When time came to start applying to colleges I felt confident in my choice of nursing. The hospital volunteer work had been so much fun that I knew I wanted to be a nurse. However, it didn't take long for that confidence to be shaken. Soon after beginning the nursing program I learned that real nursing isn't always fun. I began asking the old "Why am I here?" question all over again, but this time it was more like "How can I get out of here?"

My grades began to reflect my floundering spirit. What was the sense of studying if I didn't want to be a nurse? I dabbled in fraternity parties and other extracurricular activities, but I never really enjoyed them. I was still asking, "Why am I here?" Most of my partying friends flunked out by the end of freshman year. I squeaked by on probation. Now the question was shouting at me, "Why am I *still* here?"

During orientation week of sophomore year I ended up at a potluck dinner to meet the Nurses Christian Fellowship staff worker. The students in the NCF group had been wonderfully supportive to me when I came back to campus and discovered that none of my old gang would be returning. I figured that at least I could go to the dinner with them and give this staff worker a fair hearing. At the dinner, though, the crowd seemed awfully spiritual, and I felt a little uncomfortable. Christie, a nurse who had recently graduated, asked me, "Why did you choose nursing?"

It was a friendly question, but it increased my discomfort. Neither my negative attitude toward nursing nor my research approach to choosing a career seemed very spiritual at this point, so I mumbled something like, "In order to help people."

She cheerfully continued, "How does God fit into your decision?"

I gulped. I really didn't want to admit that I hadn't bothered to consult him. I was greatly relieved when a classmate joined us and the conversation drifted to lighter topics. But Christie's question gnawed at me—for months. I began to wonder just where God did fit in, not only with my choice of nursing as a career, but also with how I planned my life in general. It had never occurred to me that work is a call from God and that I needed to be listening to him for direction.

I was in a crisis, and my understanding of God needed to grow to meet the expanding dimensions of my life. Crisis periods obviously affect our relationships with other people. Adolescence, for example, is a time of establishing a separate identity from parents. The nature of the relationship changes from dependency to friendship and mutual respect if that separation is successful.

In a similar way, our relationship with God needs to change as we mature. God does not change, but the way we relate to him does.

As a child, I had felt close to God. He was my friend and confidant. I told him everything—my fears and my joys—and constantly talked to him about the people I loved as well as global concerns. However, although somewhere between my own familiar little world and the starving Biafrans my important decisions were coming into focus, my relationship with God did not grow to include him in the decision making. He was conveniently relegated to daily devotions and Sunday worship. I did not want the "cares of this world" to invade my quiet time.

But the Lord calls us to do more than just "come apart with me." The Christian life is not only worship and quiet time; it is daily applying what we believe to what we do. Our primary purpose in life is not to retreat but to do God's work in the world, and our relationship to God must continue to grow so that he is Lord of our lives in every dimension.

The Lord issued his call to work when he created the first human beings. The call to work is an integral part of God's Word in creation:

Then God said, "Let us make man in our image, after our likeness; and let them have dominion over the fish of the sea, and over the birds of the air, and over the cattle, and over all the earth, and over every creeping thing that creeps upon the earth." So God created man in his own image, in the image of God he created him; male and female he created them. And God . . . said to them, "Be fruitful and multiply, and fill the earth and subdue it; and have dominion over the fish of the sea and over the birds of the air and over every living thing that moves upon the earth." And God said, "Behold, I have given you every plant yielding seed which is upon the face of all the earth, and every tree with seed in its fruit; you shall have them for food." . . . And it was so. And God saw everything that he had made, and behold, it was very good. (Gen 1:26-31)

That rather comprehensive job description gives us some specific principles for planning our lives. It remains valid for Christians today, because it was issued before the Fall. It is the way God intended things to be, and it bears careful examination.

Note that the same call to work is given to both the man and the woman. They are expected to function as a team. There is no differentiation between male and female roles. The Lord does not say that the man should have dominion over the woman, but that man and woman would rule creation together.

## Dominion over Creation

Dominion is a strange concept to us who live in a democracy. Just what is dominion? Canada is called a Dominion. That means it has loose, but official, ties to the British Commonwealth. The Queen visits occasionally. However, Canada is a democracy and governs itself. Is that what Genesis 1 is talking about? Not quite.

Dominion implies control, authority and power. It carries with it great responsibility and ultimate accountability to God. The dominion that God assigns to human beings in Genesis 1 is a commission to care for the earth and its inhabitants with tenderness and love, to rule the world with justice, and to make wise use of the resources he has provided. It is a mandate to share in God's ongoing work of creation.

My husband and I have a glimpse of that kind of dominion as we care for our daughter, Janell. She responds to our love with warmth and joy. She trusts us completely. Discipline at this stage in her life is seldom necessary, but when it is, she quickly modifies her behavior to please us. At sixteen months, she dances in glee to rousing hymn tunes; she readily bows her head and folds her hands to pray and giggles when familiar names are mentioned, adding her own "Ahm" at the end of the prayer. We sense that we are participants with God in shaping her little world, so that she too can take on responsibility in his kingdom.

God intended the work of dominion to be joyful and exciting. He never meant work to be boring, frustrating or meaningless. Can you imagine the fun God must have had, and continues to have, in creating the world? Consider the infinite variety and splendor. God's power and might are emblazoned on the towering mountains and roar from the midst of the crashing ocean waves. The gentle warmth of a summer breeze whispers of his mercy, while chirping birds sing out his joy. His sense of humor delights us through the crazy antics of a monkey or the funny anatomy of the platypus or kangaroo. The regal beauty of the peacock, the sleek motion of a lion, and the riotous blast of color in autumn leaves remind us that God is the author of beauty. Chickens and cows may show God's practical nature, but in making wriggling puppies and fuzzy kittens he invites us to share in his fluff and play. By giving us dominion God allows us to join him in his creativity and care.

Exercising dominion involves making sure that all those within our realm have a fair deal. On a personal level, we are responsible to care for our immediate neighbors, to assist them in times of need and to love them—whether we like them or not. In order to do that, we have to be acquainted with the people who live around us, informed of community issues and aware of neighborhood resources such as food pantries, crisis counseling and emergency services. But we cannot stop there. Our realm goes beyond the immediate neighborhood. We are also responsible to care for those in need throughout the world.

Dominion means wisely using the resources God has given us. God's storehouse of resources presents us with a complex challenge. First, we are to use them to their fullest potential (Mt 25:14-30). The Lord wants us to enjoy his gifts, to receive them with gratitude. Have you ever given someone a gift, only to have her say, "This is much too extravagant; I can't accept it"? I have, and it made me feel rotten. Rejecting a gift usually implies rejecting the giver. Dominion requires us to accept the riches of the kingdom and to enjoy them. But the challenge is bigger than personal enjoyment. God also expects us to share those resources with others (Mt 25:31-46).

God gives us his resources in order that they may be properly distributed, not so we can hoard them (Lk 12:13-21). There is a delicate balance between enjoying what God has so richly bestowed on us and holding onto it loosely. Some years ago my roommates and I lived in a large, but modest, duplex in a changing neighborhood. It was furnished with secondhand furniture we had refinished and slipcovered ourselves. Comfortable, yes, but hardly ostentatious. We saw our home as an integral part of our ministry. It was a training center for students, volunteers and staff; it provided office space for three staff members and a secretary; and it was a second home to a constant flow of troubled people, missionaries and other Christians from around the world as well as being our own home base. But one day a student who came to our home became highly indignant. "How can you live like this?" she demanded. "Such wealth is sinful!"

I knew that my student friend had just returned from a summer missions project in Africa and was probably suffering from reverse culture shock. In comparison to the homes she had visited in Africa, our home did appear unduly luxurious. After much prayer and soul-searching, however, I finally concluded that we were being good stewards of God's gifts. Periodic soul-searching is an important part of exercising dominion. We need to ask ourselves if we are truly aware of the needs of other members of the kingdom and are doing everything possible to share with them what God has given us. We must constantly evaluate whether we are hoarding God's gifts or using them to his glory.

## Be Fruitful and Multiply

God's ongoing work of creation is more than just taking care of what already exists. By commanding Adam and Eve to "be fruitful and multiply" (Gen 1:28), he invited them to join him in creating new life. That command has often been applied exclusively to human procreation and hence considered outmoded in an age of overpopulation. Although bearing children is certainly part of the joy in creation that God intends people to share, the context of the passage indicates that there is more to it. In verse 29 God says, "I have given you every plant yielding seed which is upon the face of all the earth." In other words, he has given us the power to reproduce all he has created. He has also given us the satisfaction of seeing the fruit of our labors.

Each summer my husband and I plant a large garden. Part of the fun is finding new and unusual seeds like spaghetti squash, giant foot-long string beans and burpless cucumbers. Can you imagine the fun Adam and Eve must have had with "every plant yielding seed" at their disposal? Not only did God provide garden seeds, he also planted "seed thoughts" of discovery and creativity in people's minds. He provided abundant raw materials for us to discover and develop. Because we benefit today from the dominion exercised by those who came before us, we have much more to work with than did Adam and Eve. Our "garden" has expanded to include the depths of the seas and outer space. Laborsaving devices and limited hours on the job free us to practice dominion in expanded ways—balancing a career and a family, becoming involved in church and community service, advocating the needs of the poor and oppressed.

Just what is it that we are to multiply? Everything God created. He created food, and we are to multiply and distribute it to hungry people and animals around the world. That opens a vast area of vocational involvement from farming to manufacturing, from emergency hunger relief to teaching land conservation. God created beauty, and we can multiply it through the arts, fashion design, architecture, interior decorating, hair styling or even planting flowers around the house. God created power, and we can harness physical power to generate electricity or exercise political power to bring peace and justice in society.

When God looked over creation and pronounced it "good," he was calling the material world, as well as spiritual and relational qualities, good. That is part of the uniqueness of the Judeo-Christian world and life view. We are not called to renounce the material world. First Timothy 4:4-5 tells us, "Everything created by God is good, and nothing is to be rejected if it is received with thanksgiving; for then it is consecrated by the word of God and prayer." That attitude of thanksgiving, which spills over into service to others out of gratitude to God, is the key to our involvement with material goods.

I recently heard a prominent theologian decrying the materialism of American society. He lambasted his audience, saying that Christians are blind to the needs of the poor as we sit in our comfortable suburban communities. Then he went on to describe the poor in Central America where he was working, how they were unable to make a living wage in their own country. Finally, he presented his solution: he was teaching them to make craft items to sell to Americans. Most of the audience, propelled by guilt, made arrangements to display the trinkets for sale in their churches. Ironically, his solution contributed to the very materialism he had just accused us of creating!

In reality, the material world is good—whether we live in the suburban United States or in rural Central America. We don't have to feel guilty about the gifts God has given us. However, Jesus tells us, "Every one to whom much is given, of him will much be required" (Lk 12:48). An abundance of blessings carries a tremendous responsibility to multiply them even further for the glory of God and the benefit of those who have less.

### Subdue the Earth

When Eve called her dog in the perfect world, I'd like to think that he came right away. When I call my dog, Freckles, she gives me a blank stare and scampers off in another direction—until she knows I am really angry. Then she comes. I'd like to blame the disobedience on Freckles, but I know that it is actually my fault. I neglected to exercise dominion by taking the time and energy to train her properly when she was a puppy. Even in the Garden of Eden God had to tell Adam and Eve to subdue the earth. They had to train the animals, plant the seeds and maybe even pull the weeds.

Bringing order to creation was part of the original job description. At first that may seem rather dull and tedious, but creating order can be deeply satisfying. One reason I enjoy gardening is its tangible orderliness. While it is often difficult to measure success when working with people or abstract ideas, it is easy to look at neat, weed-free rows of corn, beans, tomatoes and peas to feel a sense of accomplishment.

Subduing the earth means bringing it under control. Wherever there is disorder, injustice, oppression or deprivation we are called to correct it. Subduing the earth requires us to live a lifestyle of service and evangelism. It means being aware of situations which need controlling and being willing to get involved. Involvement could mean anything from financial giving to changing government policies. Evangelism is an essential part of subduing the earth as well, for the only way humans will exercise true dominion is under the lordship of Christ.

God called Adam and Eve to work in a setting of abundance. They were not working in order to eat. God provided the food to sustain them while they worked. Few of us enjoy that luxury today, but an attitude is implied here which we must heed. If we work merely to put food on the table, then our lives soon become frustrating and meaningless.

Work is a lifelong calling. It is not only what we do on the job between nine and five or three and eleven, although that is part of it. Work is our partnership with God in caring for his creation. It starts from the time we first learn responsibility as a child and continues until death (not merely until retirement). Our lifework continues even when we are unemployed or when physical disabilities limit functioning. Some of the mightiest workers in God's kingdom have been prayer warriors who were totally confined to bed with debilitating illnesses. They used all that quiet time to intercede for others.

Our work may take different forms at varying periods of our lives. Choosing a major in college does not lock you into an unchangeable course. My husband, a pastor, started out as an electrical engineer. His class in seminary included a college history professor, a chemist, a florist and a tugboat pilot. Some of the more incongruous backgrounds turned out to be amazingly helpful in the pastoral ministry. My own work history has included being a clerk-typist, a nurse, a chaplain, a teacher, a library assistant, a counselor, a writer, an editor, a wife and a mother. Each of those experiences fits together as an integral part of the whole of what God has called me to do. I can look back and see a purpose and a plan not my own.

The Lord uses our interests and skills in ways we may not even be able to dream of in the present. All we are called to do is to be faithful in using the gifts and opportunities he provides. In retrospect, I can see that my research approach to choosing a lifework was more spiritual than I originally thought. For that is exactly what God calls us to do—to take stock of our interests and talents and match them with the needs surrounding us. The unifying factor in our lifework is a singleness of direction, a desire to serve God and seek his leading.

God does not call us just to build a career. He leads us into a vocation—a calling—which incorporates our total being. We are not bound by society's values or expectations. We are not limited by preconceived roles. We are not even constrained by our own limitations. We are called and empowered by God to have dominion over the earth.

## Work and the Curse

If work was meant to be so good, why don't most people find

joy and satisfaction in it? A glimpse into a few lives shows that work is often a burden, a problem or sheer drudgery.

Bob was a chemistry major in college. Upon graduation he could not find a job in his field. Now he is working as a grocery store clerk while his wife attends graduate school. He hates it.

Susan is a nurse. She went into nursing because she felt she could serve God through ministering to other people. The hospital where she works is seriously understaffed due to budget cutbacks. She feels that conditions force her to provide nursing care that is inadequate and often unsafe. She would like to change jobs, but other hospitals in the area are not hiring.

Lynn works for a Christian organization. She was delighted when the opportunity to "serve the Lord full-time" was offered to her, but now she is disillusioned. There are more interpersonal problems in this organization than she ever encountered teaching public school. She believes that some of the fund-raising schemes are clearly unethical. She has also discovered that male staff members receive much larger salaries than women in the same jobs.

George worked in industry as a computer programmer for five years. The pay was good and the work was challenging. He enjoyed his colleagues and truly looked forward to going to work each day. Then he was laid off and his world collapsed around him. His self-worth crumbled when he had to give up his apartment and move back in with his parents. Even though he knows that the loss of a major contract forced the layoffs, he can't help thinking it was his fault that he lost his job.

Marilyn never wanted to be anything but a wife and mother. When she met Tom in her sophomore year of college, she knew he was "the one." She quit school at the end of the year and married Tom. Their first year of marriage was wonderful. She decorated their home and prided herself on home-baked bread and gourmet cooking. But now, a year later, she is bored. She still is not pregnant. Tom will not consider adopting children. He gets annoyed with her fancy cooking and fussy housekeeping, complaining that he would rather have hamburgers and French fries and a little comfortable disorder around the house. She is beginning to wonder if their marriage was a mistake.

Joanne is a buyer for a major department-store chain. Her work takes her to London, Paris and Hong Kong. She loves the glamour and excitement. In comparison to her job, her marriage seemed dull and confining, so she left her husband and moved to New York. Now all her relationships are transient, and the glitter is beginning to fade.

Melanie is happy as a wife and the mother of three growing boys, but she has a hard time saying no to church and volunteer work. She is beginning to feel used. Her own housework never seems to get done. Meals are always rushed and thrown together at the last minute. She doesn't have time to do anything well because there are so many things that need doing.

A recurrent theme runs through each of these situations. It is the story of unfulfilled desires and shattered dreams. It all began in the third chapter of Genesis when Adam and Eve chose to believe the serpent rather than God. They began to dream of personal glory instead of fulfilling their God-given mission in life. For their own protection, God stopped them and pronounced a curse. That curse directly affects all of us.

To the serpent God said: "I will put enmity between you and the woman, and between your seed and her seed" (v. 15). This is both a promise and a prediction. Ultimately, the seed of the woman who will contend with Satan is Jesus Christ. However, the practical reality for the present is that all people must contend with evil in society. The sin of Adam and Eve is repeated over and over as we strive to fulfill selfish ambitions, knocking down whatever and whoever gets in our way. We are caught up in a seemingly endless power struggle, and it affects all our interpersonal relationships. We cannot escape it, even by working in a Christian environment.

We see evidence of this aspect of the curse in management and labor disputes, in tensions between family and job responsibilities, in gossip and "put-downs." It seems that the more noble the purposes of an organization, the more inevitable strife becomes. The most painful (as well as the most rewarding) working relationships I have experienced have been in the church and in Christian organizations. Satan works overtime when so much is at stake. In the curse God warns us that we are going to get hurt, emotionally and physically, as we attempt to exercise dominion in the world. An enemy is busy stirring up trouble.

There is more to the curse. God said to the woman: "I will greatly multiply your pain in childbearing; in pain you shall bring forth children, yet your desire shall be for your husband, and he shall rule over you" (v. 16). Suddenly there is a new division of labor. The man and the woman get separate, and unequal, job descriptions. The equal partnership is dissolved. The beauty and harmony of the marriage relationship is marred. One commentator describes the problem this way: " 'To love and to cherish' becomes 'To desire and to dominate.' "[1] What God designed to be the ideal working relationship has now become a source of contention. Husbands and wives compete with one another and with other distractions for one another's time and attention. It takes hard work to make a marriage into a lasting and satisfying relationship.

Problems of desire and domination also arise on the job. Sexual seduction and harassment can make a working situation unbearable. Men often receive more pay and faster promotions than women in the same jobs. Women who work outside the home usually maintain primary responsibility for child care and household chores. Women who stay at home to care for their children often receive little appreciation. It is not easy to be a woman at work.

God warned Eve about pain in childbearing. That was to be more than physical labor pains. Even before there was a "wrong crowd" for her children to join, Eve discovered that it was difficult to instill in them faith and proper values. Her son Cain murdered his brother Abel in a jealous rage.

Today we see the legacy of the curse in child abuse, spouse abuse, adolescent rebellion and family breakdowns. The added pain of illness, accidents, birth defects and infertility make childbearing frustrating, risky and sometimes overwhelming. Even parents with normal, healthy, happy children may struggle with feelings of being "trapped" and "tied down" by them. Some have responded by deciding to remain childless or to abandon the children they already have. Only yesterday the evening news reported on a mother who abandoned her two-year-old son in a shopping center. "I just couldn't take it any longer," she told police.

## A Hostile Environment

God saved the ultimate despair of the curse for Adam:

"Because you have listened to the voice of your wife, and have eaten of the tree of which I commanded you, 'You shall not eat of it,' cursed is the ground because of you; in toil you shall eat of it all the days of your life; thorns and thistles it shall bring forth to you; and you shall eat the plants of the field. In the sweat of your face you shall eat bread till you return to the ground, for out of it you were taken; you are dust, and to dust you shall return." (vv. 17-19)

Sin introduced futility and death into the world. Instead of a readily responsive garden to subdue, Adam faced a hostile environment. It would be possible to subsist, but life would now be a struggle. Most of his labor would seem meaningless and purposeless. The weeds would always grow faster than the vegetables and flowers. There would be droughts and floods, earthquakes and tornadoes, fires, plagues, insect invasions and the constant threat of war. All of life was now overshadowed by death.

In practical terms, the curse warns us that things will seldom work out the way we plan them. We all have to discover that truth for ourselves, and it is usually frustrating or outright painful. For example, when I started college I had my life all planned. I would graduate, work as a nurse for two years, and then get married and have two children. Above all, I would never move again. (I had attended twelve different schools by the time I graduated from high school.) As it turned out, I have worked for over twenty years, did not marry until I was thirty-one, and finally adopted our second child just short of my fortieth birthday. I have moved fourteen times since college. In the process I have struggled, argued with God and given up cherished hopes in utter despair, only to see God's hand at work in the midst of seeming futility. Regardless of how self-sufficient we try to be, things are ultimately beyond our control.

Each of us experiences the curse in unique ways, which means that we frequently feel alone and misunderstood. Regardless of how loving we try to be, we may end up with a collection of strained and broken relationships. In spite of how passionately we defend a just cause, there will be opposition and defeats. No matter how loyal and hard-working we try to be, we can be laid off, replaced, taken for granted, or just overlooked at promotion time. And for each of us there is death.

Although everyone has to die eventually, death is a unique experience for each person. It is the final injustice, the last enemy. It never really makes sense. Even for the person who has suffered over a long period of time and who sees death as a release, the process of dying is so dehumanizing, so unfair. Why should a person who has served God faithfully over a lifetime be subjected to the indignities of pain, foul-smelling, draining wounds, immobility, loss of bowel and bladder control and dementia? Why should an innocent child be struck with the agony of leukemia or cystic fibrosis? We are under a curse.

In the final sentence of the curse God described the vocation

from God's perspective. But we are people of promise,
live with a purpose and a hope. Ephesians 1:11-14 tells

, according to the purpose of him who accomplishes all
according to the counsel of his will, we who first hoped
rist have been destined and appointed to live for the
of his glory. In him you also, who have heard the word
th, the gospel of your salvation, and have believed in him,
sealed with the promised Holy Spirit, which is the guar-
of our inheritance until we acquire possession of it, to
raise of his glory.

have the answer to "Why am I here?" I am here to be a
God and to do those things which glorify him—to live
praise of his glory. In Christ I have an identity and a
, and this becomes the framework on which I plan my
my work. In other words, I am not here to "do my own
but to bring everything I do under the lordship of Jesus
o that it will glorify him. My relationship with Christ is
strated not only in the number of Bible studies I attend
e proper church affiliation or in mastery of spiritual dis-
, but in the way I live my total life. Religious activity is
ortant part of the Christian life, but it is only a small part
icture. Work is my primary expression of faith and praise
, my service to the neighbors he commands me to love,
ponsible stewardship of his gifts, and the most effective
of communicating the good news of salvation to the

## s Worship

Lawrence, a French monk, once said, "The time of busi-
es not with me differ from the time of prayer, and in the
nd clatter of my kitchen, while several persons are at the
me calling for different things, I possess God in as great
llity as if I were upon my knees at the blessed sacrament."[2]

we choose if we decide to live apart from him: "In the sweat of
your face you shall eat bread till you return to the ground, for out
of it you were taken; you are dust, and to dust you shall return."
That is the more realistic version of "Eat, drink and be merry, for
tomorrow we die." The pursuit of pleasure leads only to emptiness and despair. Under the curse we are locked into a struggle
to survive, a struggle that we will inevitably lose.

Thanks be to God that the Bible does not stop with the third
chapter of Genesis. The story goes on.

# 2
# What Wo
# Can Be

T HE GOSPEL BLOWS THE fresh air of rede
of the curse. We have been re-called by Go
He not only gives us a new start, he also
do his will (Rom 1:16). We aren't quite
Eden; we are not yet perfect, but we are al
ing to God's original purpose and plan. Th
thistles to contend with, but we know that
ary frustrations. God is accomplishing his
in heaven and earth, and he has called us—
to be his children through Jesus Christ. We
work again. We can now be sure that, if our
with God's will, it will ultimately succeed.

That is not merely "the power of positive
fail. We do not always perceive the will of
13:12). We are not always able to understar

stances
and we
us:
In hi
thing
in C
prais
of tr
were
ante
the
Now I
child o
to the
purpos
life an
thing,"
Christ
demon
or in t
cipline
an imp
of the
to Go
my re
means
world.

**Work**
Brothe
ness c
noise
same
tranqu

As a Christian finds a new identity in Christ, work becomes the natural outgrowth of that re-creation (Eph 2:8-9). Just as a husband and wife try to do those things which please each other, Christians seek to glorify God through works. Verbal expressions of love and praise are important, but the true test of commitment comes through action. As James says, "So faith by itself, if it has no works, is dead" (2:17).

Marriage, like life in Christ, is a full-time relationship. I am not married only when I am at home, but also when I am at work and even when I am out of town. Marriage affects all my plans and all my relationships with other people. Sometimes it gets rather complicated. I cannot schedule meetings, agree to attend an out-of-town event or make decisions which will affect our life together without first consulting my husband. Sometimes I know he will be pleased if I accept a certain invitation, but I still check with him to make sure it will not conflict with a higher priority. Our relationship with God demands similar interaction. If our work is truly to be worship, it must be a day-by-day response to his will and grace.

The apostle Paul in Romans 12:1-2 described this dynamic: "I appeal to you therefore, brethren, by the mercies of God, to present your bodies as a living sacrifice, holy and acceptable to God, which is your spiritual worship. Do not be conformed to this world but be transformed by the renewal of your mind, that you may prove what is the will of God, what is good and acceptable and perfect."

The concept was revolutionary. According to many of the popular religions in Paul's day (and to a great extent in our own), the body was evil and distracting. True worship meant denying the body and focusing on the divine spark which was believed to dwell within a person. Most people would certainly not see the body as "holy and acceptable to God." But in Christ the whole person, including the body, has been redeemed. That demands a response in our thoughts and in our behavior.

*Worship* in the New Testament essentially means "service." The same word is used to describe the labor of slaves or hired servants.[3] Jesus illustrated the concept by telling the story of the good Samaritan (Lk 10:30-37). He also explained that worship not only means being reconciled to God, but also requires us to forgive others (Mt 5:23-24; 6:14-15). He further taught that worship is not something we do only in a holy place, but that it is done "in spirit and truth" (Jn 4:24). Singing hymns and praising God with our lips is only the beginning of worship. If it does not lead to doing work which reflects the nature of God, we are not worshiping in spirit and truth. Faith must affect every fiber of our being, every hour of the day, every relationship and commitment, in order to exist in spirit and truth.

A friend once explained to me that she had decided to tithe her time as well as her income. That meant she spent ten per cent of her time doing something religious. At first, that seemed like a wonderful idea—expecially since she intended to use part of her time-tithe to do volunteer work for Nurses Christian Fellowship and I was her staff worker. But gradually I realized that ninety per cent of my friend's time was not committed to the Lord at all. She had carefully boxed God into a ten-per-cent time slot.

In contrast, Paul appeals to us to be completely transformed in our thinking, rather than comfortably conforming to the world. That involves carefully evaluating the filters through which we view our values, goals and day-to-day activities and relationships. Our "spiritual worship" includes what we do on the job, how we spend our free time, the education we pursue, the way we treat other people and the way we measure success. It is so easy to slip into conformity with the world in each of these areas that we seldom recognize it happening.

On the job, we are subtly drawn into conforming by the attitudes and actions of the people around us. It is difficult to abstain from the petty dishonesty that often pervades the workplace. Using the photocopy machine for personal business, taking a few pens home in your pocket, or stretching lunch and coffee breaks beyond their time limits seem so minor—especially when everybody else does it. On another level, we conform to the world when we are silent about our beliefs and values for fear of rejection. We also conform when we give in to negative forces instead of trying to effect change.

For example, Sue lasted four weeks on her first job. The competition, backbiting and general negative tenor overwhelmed her, reinforcing her own sense of inadequacy. She soon found another job in a nearby town. There she adjusted well and gained confidence in her skills with the encouragement of her colleagues. After about six months a new supervisor took over her team. The newcomer was deceitful and abrasive. Sue's former encouragers decided that it was easier to ask for a transfer than to confront the woman about her offensive behavior. Perhaps Sue could have either helped the woman to change or stayed to encourage newcomers so that they would be able to withstand the supervisor's negative influence. Instead she joined the crowd and decided to resign.

Conforming to the world in our free time takes many forms, some more obvious than others. Mike, for instance, came home from work each evening and switched on the television. He ate his dinner in front of the TV, usually falling asleep on the sofa afterward. When he awoke around nine o'clock he seldom had the energy to start any new projects, so he went to bed. Despite all the sleep he got, he always felt tired. He refused to become involved with activities at church or in the community because he felt he just did not have the energy to do anything more.

On the other hand Meg prided herself on her full calendar. She led a high-school Bible study every Wednesday morning at six o'clock, took the teens on weekend retreats, taught Sunday school, sang in the choir, was active in the singles group at church and attended postgraduate classes two evenings a week. Since many of her commitments fell on the same dates, people who depended on her were often disappointed. Meg became so caught up in her activities that she seldom spent time in prayer and Bible study—unless it was with a group. On the job, Meg chattered continuously about all her Christian involvements, often neglecting her work. Even though her frenetic activities had an outwardly Christian flavor, Meg was conforming to the world's "rat race" mentality.

Education is a great conformer. Students seldom stop to question whether theories and techniques taught in class have a philosophical basis which conflicts with the Scriptures, especially when they are presented in scientific garb. Big controversial issues such as evolution or humanism or sex education may trouble a few Christians, but most questionable areas slip by unnoticed. For instance, Jack, a Christian graduate student, took a course on stress reduction where he learned yoga exercises and transcendental meditation. He "Christianized" the practices by putting Christian terminology in place of what was taught, but he never considered the philosophical foundation for the techniques.

Mark conformed in another way. He believed God had called him to be a pastor, but he dropped out of seminary after the first semester. He constantly disagreed with his professors and intensely disliked studying. He spent most of his time volunteering at a rescue mission and working in a small country church, and he accused his classmates of avoiding "real ministry" by spending so much time on campus. "Education is just a headtrip," he commented. "All I need is my Bible and the Holy Spirit." By rejecting the hard work of studying and by refusing to be open to new ideas, Mark was conforming to the world's attitude of "do your own thing" instead of functioning as a member of the body of Christ.

We also conform by using people or neglecting them instead of loving and caring for them. Elaine, for example, felt embarrassed about witnessing to strangers, but the Bible school she attended required each student to present the gospel to a min-imum of six people each week. Elaine became a hit-and-run evangelist. She would go to the city park and rattle off a mem-orized outline of the gospel to the first six people who looked friendly, then run back to the dorm, relieved that her quota for the week was met.

Shirley, bright and energetic, quickly rose up the steps of the corporate ladder by spending most of her waking hours at work. In the process she grew emotionally distant from her husband and children. The children often went straight from the day-care center to the baby sitter. Shirley would not see them awake for several days at a time. However, she measured success by the world's standards, and she knew she was successful because a gold vice-president sign graced her office door.

The influences which lead us into conformity are usually sub-tle. They may be disguised as virtues. There is nothing wrong with being successful in a career; there is certainly nothing wrong with evangelism or serving as a volunteer in Christian activities; but the person whose mind is transformed by Jesus Christ will consider attitudes as well as actions and will be concerned about how both attitudes and actions affect other people.

How does this transformation take place? Note that Paul tells us to "be transformed by the renewal of your mind." He does not say "transform yourself." Transformation is a work of God's grace and power within us. However, we have a responsibility to par-ticipate in the process. We must be open to allowing God to change us. We need to renew our minds through studying the Scriptures, spending time in prayer and interacting with other Christians. That interaction involves more than casual encounters. It means submitting ourselves to other Christians who know us well—mature Christians who can "preach the word, be urgent in season and out of season, convince, rebuke, and exhort, be un-failing in patience and in teaching" (2 Tim 4:2). Such submission is a mutual commitment to and caring for one another, not a mindless obedience. It is a lifelong process whereby the rough edges of the "old nature" are chipped away and we become more and more like Christ (2 Cor 3:18; 4:16). It takes place in the context of everyday life and work.

## Work as Service

If work is a response of worship and worship is essentially service, then the type of work we do is important to God. Jesus provided clear guidelines when he summed up the commandments: "You shall love the Lord your God with all your heart, and with all your soul, and with all your mind. . . . You shall love your neighbor as yourself" (Mt 22:37, 39). Our work must be a service to God and to our neighbors. Theologian T. A. Kantonen explains, "Christian saintliness is not a monastic withdrawal from the world for the sake of sinlessness for oneself. It is self-forgetting service to others by the power of him who uses imperfect instruments to accomplish his holy purposes."⁴

Christian service does not necessarily mean going to a foreign mission field or becoming a pastor or doing some other "full-time Christian work." It means that whatever we do should be in keeping with God's purposes and plan. It must be a means of showing God's love to our neighbors. It must reflect God's righteousness and power. We are to go out into the world as "salt" and "light," but we are not to be *of* the world (Mt 5:13-14; Jn 17:15-16). In other words, we are to work side by side with non-Christians without getting caught up in their philosophies and values. We are to work within society to preserve human dignity and worth, to strive for justice, to care for the suffering and oppressed, and to communicate the good news of God's love and forgiveness through Jesus Christ. Often that means we will get stuck with the dirty work. Sometimes it will lead us into conflict with supervisors and colleagues. It may mean standing up for unpopular causes or people. It may lead to ridicule or threaten our job security.

For some, it may involve playing along with the system in order to gain enough power to change that system. A university professor once told me, "the pressures to get a doctorate and to publish scholarly articles are just a matter of educational politics in my field. It doesn't have anything to do with being a good teacher—but I had to do those things myself before I could criticize with any credibility."

Brother Lawrence could serve God and his neighbor by working in the kitchen. Christians can serve in business, politics, engineering, the arts, the helping professions, education and industry. Opportunities to serve are endless. No area of society should be left uninfiltrated by the salt and light of a Christian presence. However, Christians working in particularly "worldly" settings may face criticism and misunderstanding from other Christians. In such cases they may begin to feel out of place both in the church and in the secular world. A support group of Christians in similar work can be a tremendous encouragement (see appendix for a listing of such groups).

Perhaps more important than the type of work in which a Christian serves is his or her attitude and motivation for that work. A person can appear to be making great sacrifices by going to the mission field while operating from a motive of personal glory and prestige. On the other hand, another Christian may mount a high-pressure political campaign, travel the party circuit and appear to be seeking personal power and acclaim—all in order to make important changes in government policy which will benefit underprivileged people. Motivation for organizing a union can range from materialistic greed to a deep concern for justice and fair labor practices. What is right for one Christian may be inappropriate, or outright sinful, for another. A person's attitude and motivation can make the difference.

Servant attitudes are not very popular in our society. Even the traditional serving professions like nursing are trying to shake off the servant image. Christians are called to buck the trend in the world around us: "For you were called to freedom, brethren; only do not use your freedom as an opportunity for the flesh, but through love be servants of one another" (Gal 5:13). Servanthood does not necessarily mean being a doormat, but it is a basic attitude of loving, caring and willingness to go the extra mile when necessary. It is not easy to be different. A person who is willing to be a servant may be resented by coworkers if they feel pressured to perform equally. At the same time, they may be more than willing to unload all their unpleasant tasks on the uncomplaining servant. For Jesus, servanthood meant death on the cross—and that was his lifework.

## Work as Stewardship

Christian service restores us to our Genesis 1 calling to be stewards of God's creation. In biblical times, a steward was a person entrusted with the maintenance and management of a household or even a kingdom. The steward acted on behalf of the owner. It was a position of great trust and prestige. Joseph is a good example of a steward. Pharaoh "set him over all the land of Egypt" (Gen 41:43) and gave him control over all his people and possessions. Pharaoh was still the ruler, but Joseph was in charge. He wisely managed Pharaoh's resources and governed the people so there was order and plenty during a time of terrible famine.

The Lord has appointed us to a similar position. We are stewards of his creation, of the gifts he has given us and of the gospel. Our job is to be faithful with the resources he has entrusted to us and to care for our neighbors so they will not fall victim to famine. That famine can be a literal scarcity of food and shelter, or it can be a famine of power resulting in oppression and injustice, or it can be the famine described in Amos 8:11, "not a famine of bread, nor a thirst for water, but of hearing the words of the LORD."

Stewardship of creation has become a huge and overwhelming task in an age when we can flip on the television and see wars, earthquakes, floods and other major disasters flash before us in living color. We want to help, but do not know where to begin. We give sacrificially to aid the victims and later hear that church funds have been diverted to buy weapons or subsidize rebellions. We begin to wonder who can be trusted and are tempted to give up trying. We read that, despite our good intentions, we are exploiting poor people in other countries by eating bananas and drinking coffee.[5] We hear that natural resources are being depleted, rare species of animals becoming extinct, drinking supplies being contaminated. Yet we feel powerless to effect meaningful change. Where does a Christian begin to exercise stewardship?

Obviously, we cannot take on the whole world by ourselves. But there is hope. Romans 8:18-21 tells us: "The sufferings of this present time are not worth comparing with the glory that is to be revealed to us. For the creation waits with eager longing for the revealing of the sons of God; . . . because the creation itself will be set free from its bondage to decay and obtain the glorious liberty of the children of God."

We are what the world has been waiting for! The church, operating in the power of the resurrection, can begin to set creation free. We do it through working together with other Christians. Even though the media report abuses in the use of church funds, they are rare. The church has an amazingly good record for alleviating human suffering. Most hospitals and social service agencies around the world can trace their beginnings to concerned Christians who cared enough to get involved. Most relief work in major disasters is handled through Christian agencies. The church has taken the lead in feeding the hungry, caring for the refugees and advocating for the poor in the world. We can participate by giving financially, serving on the front lines, putting pressure on governments and others in power, and living a lifestyle consistent with our beliefs.

The church's record for stewardship over natural resources is

not so glowing. Part of the problem is a distorted view of stewardship. Rather than tending the earth for its own benefit, we have
too often selfishly exploited it. Another part of the problem, at
least until recent years, was ignorance. Most people seemed to
think God had lavished on us an endless supply of resources to
be used with abandon. Only recently did we discover that the
supply is limited. It is time to begin to protect our environment
and care for that which has been entrusted to us.

Stewardship is an individual responsibility as well as a corporate one. We are stewards of the gifts God has bestowed on us
personally; we are to use them in the context of the body of
Christ—and the world. First Peter 4:10 tells us: "As each has
received a gift, employ it for one another, as good stewards of
God's varied grace." God has created us as unique persons with
varying talents and interests. It is our job as stewards to discover
what we do well and enjoy doing in order to do it for God's glory.
For one person that may mean tracking a rare species of bird in
the jungles of South America; for another it may lead to produc-
ing quality television programming; for yet another it could involve leading children's Bible studies and being available to people who need a caring friend.

In the process of discovering and using our gifts, we must keep
in mind the admonition in 1 Corinthians 12:4-7: "Now there are
varieties of gifts, but the same Spirit; and there are varieties of
service, but the same Lord; and there are varieties of working, but
it is the same God who inspires them all in every one. To each
is given the manifestation of the Spirit for the common good."
The chapter goes on to show that there is no hierarchy of functions. Regardless of the esteem accorded by human standards, in
God's sight each role is equal.

A friend I have known since we were both single and with
whom I have shared many common goals recently confided, "I
feel so guilty when I see the books you have written. All I have
managed to do in the last ten years is raise four children." She

also has a beautiful ministry to the women and children in her neighborhood. She actively shares her faith, supports the grieving, bears the burdens of the suffering and opens her home to other people's children in need of love. I am tempted to feel guilty because I have had to shut out many of those involvements in order to have time to write. But we cannot compare ourselves to one another to determine the standards for our work.

Neither do we have to feel locked into using one gift or set of gifts throughout our whole lives. My friend, who was an excellent and beloved teacher before her marriage, is developing other gifts as her children mature. My own lifestyle and interests are changing now that we have two active children. We live in a constantly changing world. God gives us gifts to equip us to meet the challenges that confront us daily, to give us stability as individuals and as members of the body of Christ as we "grow up in every way into him who is the head, into Christ, from whom the whole body, joined and knit together by every joint with which it is supplied, when each part is working properly, makes bodily growth and upbuilds itself in love" (Eph 4:15-16).

Looking at the seasons of our lives as an unfolding of God's plan rather than as random forces tossing us to and fro imbues life with a sense of excitement and purpose. We are stewards in constant interaction with God, receiving from him wisdom, strength and ability to do the work he calls us to do in each season. Life certainly is never boring when a person is alive in Christ.

## Work as Evangelism

Our stewardship does not end with physical and temporal concerns. We are also stewards of the gospel. According to 1 Corinthians 4:1, "This is how one should regard us, as servants of Christ and stewards of the mysteries of God." The Christian's work in the world is evangelism.

The work of evangelism is one of the most misunderstood

aspects of our calling as Christians. Even the mention of doing evangelism at work causes panic in most of us. Our nagging fear of evangelism usually causes us to move to one of two extremes. Either we hide our faith and quietly go about our business hoping our good works will speak for themselves, or we become obnoxious and try to convert people without being sensitive to them as individuals. Neither end of the spectrum is true evangelism.

Evangelism, of course, is telling the good news of God's love and forgiveness offered to us through Jesus Christ. What we do tells as much about the gospel as what we say, for it authenticates the message. If the work we do is inconsistent with the character of God, then the message becomes distorted—it no longer comes across as good news.

Early in my nursing career I worked with another Christian nurse who felt compelled to witness to every patient immediately before surgery. She would go into the person's room just before the preoperative medication was given and ask, "If you die on the operating table, will you go to heaven or hell?" Most patients never heard anything beyond the first seven words. They panicked. Several refused to go to the operating room. None of them received Christ. In her enthusiasm for evangelism the nurse often forgot important preoperative procedures like removing jewelry, dentures and nail polish. This created dangerous situations. After ample warnings the nurse was finally fired. She believed she had been persecuted for her faith and was fired because of the "offense of the gospel." In reality, she was dismissed for her shoddy, unsafe and insensitive nursing care.

Jesus tells us, "You are the light of the world. A city set on a hill cannot be hid. Nor do men light a lamp and put it under a bushel, but on a stand, and it gives light to all in the house. Let your light so shine before men, that they may see your good works and give glory to your Father who is in heaven" (Mt 5:14-16). In other words, our work and our witness go hand in hand.

Our first responsibility as Christians is to do our work well. In so doing we earn the right to tell why.

In another hospital I worked with several Christian nurses and quite a few skeptics. The Christians quietly but openly set about meeting the spiritual needs of patients. They did this with sensitivity and gentleness. Frequently a nurse would report, "I prayed with Mrs. Jones at bedtime and she seemed to settle down after that." When one of the skeptics encountered a patient who wanted to discuss spiritual things, she would find one of the Christians and say, "I think Mr. Hall needs to talk to you." It was not at all unusual for a coffee-break conversation to center around the effect of prayer, the sovereignty of God or other spiritual topics which provided an open door to share our faith. The light set on a stand drew skeptics like moths.

As stewards of the gospel we are told to "conduct yourselves wisely toward outsiders, making the most of the time. Let your speech always be gracious, seasoned with salt, so that you may know how you ought to answer every one" (Col 4:5-6). First, we are to conduct ourselves wisely. Rather than being naively irrelevant in our evangelism, we need to be aware of the ways of the world and the needs of the people around us. Then we can make the most of the time available by explaining the gospel in terms that make sense to our colleagues and associates. That requires spending enough time with them to learn their lingo and assess their felt needs. Sometimes it means wading through a mire of language and behavior most Christians would find shocking and immoral—without passing judgment—until a person is able to express feelings of emptiness and a need for God.

Maribeth constantly bragged about her promiscuous relationships with men. Sue, a Christian colleague, began to see a hurting person under Maribeth's tough exterior, and she befriended her. At one point Maribeth said to Sue, "You don't sleep around, do you? How come?"

Sue was tempted to preach, but instead she said, "Well, I believe God made us with a need to experience the trust and security of having only one faithful sexual partner."

Maribeth became quiet for a moment, then changed the subject. Later, she sought out Sue to tell her, "Hey, what you said was really profound. Do you know how lonely it is to go from bed to bed knowing that none of those guys really cares about me? I just don't know how to change. What else does God say about our needs?"

By acting wisely Sue won the right to be heard. It took a while for Sue to get around to sharing the gospel, but she had made the most of the time because, when she did share, it was effective. She spoke graciously and gently, yet without compromising her own position. Maribeth became a Christian.

Work as evangelism can lead beyond the bounds of one-to-one relationships. Proclaiming the gospel in the world involves permeating the structures of society with the salt and light of Jesus Christ. For some Christians that may mean running for political office. Former president Jimmy Carter won the ear, and the respect, of a variety of influential people when he spoke about his faith. His work was powerful evangelism—even to people who disagreed with him. Other Christians who see their work as evangelism may examine the theoretical frameworks for their professions and propose Christian alternatives. Christians in the health professions have seen a rapid invasion of Eastern and occult philosophy beginning to shape current practice. In response, they are writing articles from a Christian perspective for professional journals, providing workshops and seminars for continuing education, and teaching courses on spiritual needs from a biblical viewpoint. Still other Christians have chosen more radical involvement and have worked against repressive governments because they believe the gospel of Jesus Christ compels them to let the oppressed go free.

Work as evangelism is both a personal and a corporate responsibility. It is living out the good news of Jesus Christ in the world.

It is a response of faith. It is caring
is responsibly tending the world's
God has given us to the fullest. It
pose and plan to unite all things in
of his glory.

# 3
# Is God's Call
# Sexist?

DOES GOD CALL WOMEN to the ministry? Few Christians would deny that he calls women to a general ministry, but many are less sure about the specific pastoral ministry. Even in denominations which encourage women to go into the ministry, giving careful biblical rationale, women pastors may have difficulty finding a congregation. Often it is other women in congregations who are most adamantly opposed to calling a woman pastor.

Does God call men to nursing? The idea breeds suspicion in some people's minds. Why would a man go into nursing, they ask. Wasn't he smart enough to get into medical school? Is he having problems with his masculine identity? Is it safe to allow him to care for women patients? (Interestingly, no one raises the last question about male physicians or asks whether it is safe for female nurses to care for men.)

Male and female role distinctions, though often confining, provide a great deal of safety and stability. All of us grow up with certain role expectations for men and women, based on our own experience. Though we may consciously set out to have an egalitarian marriage, we unconsciously expect our spouses to be just like Mom or Dad. My husband and I spent our first year of marriage discovering those little quirks. I would look at the overflowing kitchen wastebasket and fume because Jim didn't empty it. He couldn't understand why I let it get so full. But when I was growing up, my dad always emptied the trash. In his parents' home, the kitchen was his mom's domain and no one dared tread in it uninvited. Since then we have worked out our own set of mutually agreeable role expectations. It makes life much easier to be able to assume that certain jobs will get done without negotiating each time over who will do them.

Over the course of a marriage, as in the history of nations, churches and the job market, situations change and roles have to be renegotiated in order to be useful. Changing patterns which have become second nature is always uncomfortable and often painful, but not changing can be stifling and unfair.

Mike and Joanne had a traditional marriage. She stayed home to cook, clean and care for the children while he worked as a plant supervisor. During a period of increased pressure at the factory Mike worked a great deal of overtime, so Joanne took on all the household responsibilities. Then Mike was laid off. Joanne quickly found a job as a store clerk, but when she came home from work exhausted, she found a mountain of housework awaiting her. After a week of feeling overwhelmed, she bitterly asked Mike why he had not chipped in to help with the housework. He was shocked at her anger. It simply had not occurred to him that she needed help—especially since he felt he was doing more than his share by watching the children all day while she was at work. The previously convenient roles no longer fit; they had to be renegotiated.

Changes in society, the work force and the church may also

mean that comfortable old roles need renegotiating. For instance, although women pastors have not been commonly accepted in American evangelical churches, large numbers of women missionaries serve those churches in pastoral roles overseas. Many of these women, on returning to the States, have felt out of place and unappreciated in their male-dominated churches. We see another example in nursing, which began during the Crusades as a male occupation practiced by an order of knights. When Florence Nightingale took off to nurse the wounded of the Crimean War, she boldly stepped out of her role as a proper lady of the times. Her impact is still felt: today nursing is seen as primarily a woman's role.

Role expectations can provoke deep emotions. Our view of the "way things ought to be" is usually a mixture of theology, values, piety and tradition—in reverse order of importance. While we would like to think that our theology informs our values, piety and tradition, the opposite is more often the case. We defend our position by saying, "Jesus Christ is the same yesterday and today and for ever" (Heb 13:8). Yes, Jesus is the same, but everything else is transient. We must live in a dynamically growing relationship with him in order to apply our faith to changing circumstances. We cannot even read the Scriptures without the veil of tradition covering our eyes and the dim mirror of our culture reflecting back what we want to see. However, with the two-edged sword of the Word the Holy Spirit can break through and speak afresh in our own day, freeing us from the wooden roles we create for ourselves.

## Women in Scripture

The roles of men and women in the Scriptures can be hotly debated. I do not want to add more fuel to the fire. But personally, I find the Bible to be amazingly pro-woman. A cursory look at examples of male and female roles in Scripture is revealing. First of all, the fact that women are mentioned at all is significant for a culture that did not even count the women when totalling the number in a crowd. But what is more surprising is that throughout Scripture we find men and women serving in similar capacities (though not in equal numbers). We have already seen that Adam and Eve received the same job description to exercise dominion over creation. Moses' sister, Miriam, played a large role in saving his life when he was an infant, and then she served as a respected member of the leadership team as he led the people out of Egypt (Mic 6:4). Deborah (Judg 4:1—5:31) served among a succession of male judges in Israel. G. T. Manley, in the *New Bible Dictionary,* called these judges "a type of Christ, who came to be our Savior, is with us as our Leader, and will come to be our Judge."[6] Esther, Queen of Persia and a Jew, used her position of influence to protect the Jewish people (Est 2—9).

The ideal wife portrayed in Proverbs 31:10-31 is a fascinating study of male and female roles. The wife is involved in merchandising, manufacturing, administration, farming, real estate, the garment industry, teaching and philanthropy. All the while, she cares for her family and integrates her calling as a wife and mother with her work in the world. Apparently the family budget depends upon her income (v. 11). Her husband, a government official (perhaps the king), is proud of her and feels secure (not threatened) because of her accomplishments. She sounds like a contemporary woman.

Women, as well as men, followed Jesus and shared in his ministry. Jesus affirmed their right to do so when he told Martha that Mary's choice, to sit at his feet rather than help in the kitchen, was the "good portion, which shall not be taken away from her" (Lk 10:42).

Paul told Timothy, "Let a woman learn in silence with all submissiveness. I permit no woman to teach or to have authority over men; she is to keep silent" (1 Tim 2:11-12). However, we have strong evidence in the rest of the New Testament that this was the exception more than the rule in Paul's own ministry. In fact, the very same epistle gives instructions for women leaders in the church (1 Tim 3:11), and Paul later credited Timothy's mother and grandmother with teaching the younger man the Scriptures (2 Tim 1:5; 3:15). In Romans 16, Paul named eight women in ministry. Phoebe (v. 1) is called a *diakonos,* or minister, who is in a position of prominence. The word translated "helper" in regard to Phoebe (RSV) is translated "leader," "governor" or "protector" when applied to men. Both Prisca and Aquila (v. 3) are called "fellow workers." They jointly instructed Apollos (a man) in the faith and traveled with Paul on his missionary journey to Syria (Acts 18). In Philippians 4:2-3 Paul appeals to two women, Euodia and Syntyche, to "agree in the Lord," then goes on to explain that "they have labored side by side with me in the gospel together with Clement and the rest of my fellow workers."

The crowning statement in the Scriptures about God's role expectations is made in Galatians 3:28: "There is neither Jew nor Greek, there is neither slave nor free, there is neither male nor female; for you are all one in Christ Jesus." We are free to be whatever God calls us to be. However, we still live in a fallen world, so there is a constant tension at work. Part of that tension comes through in Galatians 5. "For freedom Christ has set us free; stand fast therefore, and do not submit again to a yoke of slavery" (v. 1). "For you were called to freedom, brethren; only do not use your freedom as an opportunity for the flesh, but through love be servants of one another" (v. 13). We are free to do what God calls us to do and should not allow other people's role expectations to constrain us. On the other hand, we are not to use our freedom to serve our own pride at others' expense.

## The Limits of Freedom

Maryann entered medical school with a chip on her shoulder. She was there to prove a point. No one was going to tell her what to do. Seeing the power and prestige of male physicians in her community, she set out to achieve equal footing—immediately.

Although she did well academically, she refused to do the menial tasks required of medical students and was soon dismissed. She then brought a legal suit against the school, claiming sexual discrimination.

Thirty-year-old Joe was director of nursing in a large hospital. He explained to a friend, "I chose nursing as a career because I knew I could get to the top fast in a primarily female profession."

In the last ten years the helping professions have suffered because they are viewed as "women's work"; hence, as servile and demeaning. Capable, intelligent women are being steered into more prestigious jobs such as medicine, law and business management. Traditionally male professions and jobs are seen as more appealing.

There is no reason why all positions for which a person is qualified should not be equally available to men and women; however, for the Christian, motivation for seeking a particular role is extremely important. No legitimate work should be considered degrading. We work to serve, not to prove a point or to gain personal power and prestige. One of the limits of our freedom in Christ is that we must avoid serving human pride. That puts us in direct opposition to the trends in our culture, but it also frees us to consider a whole new world of opportunities.

Don and Lucille believed God was calling them to the ministry. At first, Don attended seminary and Lucille took care of the children, teaching part-time to support the family. But Don was a poor student, so Lucille began to help him with his papers and coach him for exams. She thoroughly enjoyed studying theology. In the meantime, Don began to realize that he enjoyed keeping house and playing with the children. They switched roles. Lucille matriculated in seminary, and Don dropped out to be a "househusband" and eventually to start a day-care center. Unconventional, yes, but Don and Lucille have each found a ministry where their gifts can be used to the maximum.

A second limitation on our Christian freedom comes when our behavior causes disharmony in the body of Christ. In this area we walk a fine line. There are times when church people need to be made a little uncomfortable about sexual discrimination. Some rules and policies regarding women are merely cultural and have little or no basis in Scripture. Others may be firmly based on one particular interpretation of Scripture, but there is room for strong disagreement. In such cases it may be entirely appropriate to work gently, but firmly, for change. However, in many such situations it may be necessary to work within the system in order to minister effectively.

Evelyn belonged to a church which forbade women to teach men. When she returned from the mission field with an exciting report about her work, she was allowed to speak only to women's meetings. The men heard from their wives about Evelyn's stimulating message and wanted to hear her speak, too. Finally, they set up a loudspeaker so the men could sit in the next room and eavesdrop while Evelyn spoke to the women.

At first Evelyn was annoyed. She had been teaching men on the mission field. In fact, she was the only qualified Bible teacher on her station. The whole idea of putting the men in the next room seemed ludicrous, but by working within the rules she eventually enabled the men to see the absurdity of their policy. On her next furlough she was invited to speak to the entire congregation.

The principle involved here is the one Paul applied to slaves as well as to women (see Eph 6:5-8; Col 3:22—4:1; Tit 2:9-10 on slavery; and 1 Cor 11:2-16; 1 Tim 2:11 on women). He was not necessarily condoning slavery (although these verses were used to justify slavery in the United States) or the subjugation of women, but was recognizing that the message of the gospel is bigger than cultural constraints. We can be free in Christ without being completely free from established roles and expectations. It takes time—sometimes centuries—for the reality of what it means to be "one in Christ" to permeate even Christian society. We will not know full equality until Christ returns.

Neither will we know freedom from sexual seduction and harassment in this life. It is often unconscious, and it happens among Christians as well as out in the secular world. Years ago an article in the Inter-Varsity staff handbook warned that staff men and women should avoid riding in cars together or working together too closely. We all got a big chuckle out of it, and the article became an in-group joke. Later, when I experienced great difficulty controlling my warm feelings toward a male colleague, I realized the wisdom of that warning. We finally had to agree to work together only in groups.

Paul had to warn Timothy to flee youthful lusts (2 Tim 2:22). Being Christian and therefore one in Christ does not change our anatomy and physiology. We need to be aware of our limitations when working with the opposite sex. The problem becomes more intense in settings where colleagues do not share a Christian view of morality. Modest dress and behavior will help, but they will not entirely insulate us from temptation. Sometimes the only solution is to flee—to get out of the situation.

## Two-Career Families

Another limitation on our freedom from sexual stereotypes comes when exercising freedom causes disruption in the family. Careful preparation and good communication need to precede any major role changes. The impact of one spouse's sudden decision to start a new job—or to resign from a job—can be traumatic to the entire family, especially if it is a sudden, unilateral decision.

When Bob and Margerie were married they both intended to remain in their careers. Two weeks after each child was born Margerie was back to work. A live-in housekeeper cared for the children, cooked and cleaned. The family budget required two incomes. Then suddenly Margerie decided she wanted to be a full-time homemaker. She came home from work one day and men students in exchange for sexual favors.

the gospel is distorted by sexual prejudice or people used or justice is clearly at stake, we must stand firm om God has given—even if it causes conflict. Taking sial stand is always painful. We open ourselves to jection and even ostracism. It is often difficult to main- rspective, especially when other Christians with equal ppose us. Temptations mount to attack others person- nd together with like-minded crusaders and create a to retreat altogether. Open dialog without emotional is difficult when sexual roles and stereotypes are ques- ey are too much a part of our identities. Men and no feel comfortable with the status quo may feel threat- n it is challenged. Any attempt to bring change must in prayer—not only for success, but also for gentleness om. Through it all, an awareness of the sovereignty of the security of knowing that our worth and identity m him will keep the struggle balanced.

told Bob that she had resigned her job. A major upheaval ensued.

Two-career families are becoming more and more common today. Most young couples do not even consider the traditional arrangement where the wife stays home while her husband goes off to work—at least not until there are young children in the family. Child care and housework are no longer as time consuming as they once were. Smaller families, modern conveniences and longer lifespans mean that mothers have more time to give to other pursuits. There is no reason for women to stay home and bake bread just to keep busy. But problems may develop in two-career marriages, and we need to be aware of the warning signals.

Jill and Oscar met and married in law school. After passing the bar they went into law practice together. Before long they were locked into intense competition with each other. Finally they decided to specialize in different areas. Their relationship smoothed out for a while; then Jill began making more money than Oscar and their competition took another form. When Jill became pregnant she reduced her working hours and her income. The marriage relationship drastically improved. Jill decided not to go back to full-time law practice. When their daughter started school Jill volunteered at a free legal clinic in the city.

Competition can be a serious problem in some marriages. Ingrained cultural standards may grate at a man's self-image when his wife earns more than he does. Intellectually, this may not make sense, but emotionally the problem remains. For the Christian, commitment to a spouse must take precedence over career goals—and usually it is the wife who bends.

Darla and Mike described their marriage relationship as "two ships passing in the night." Darla, a nurse, worked nights, including every other weekend. Mike, an architectural engineer, worked days, but had frequent evening meetings with clients. He also attended choir practice and at least one meeting a week at church. They seldom saw each other.

Hectic schedules can devastate a marriage. There may be times when spouses must work on conflicting schedules, but in many cases we simply fail to plan creatively. Mike and Darla were trying to save money for the down payment on a house. The only job openings at a nearby hospital were on the 11—7 shift, so Darla felt she had no choice. Eventually she discovered several positions available in doctor's offices which required no weekend work. The pay was not as high, but the benefit of having more time with Mike offset the loss in pay. Darla was able to join the choir with Mike, and Mike resigned from one church committee.

Another serious consideration in exercising our freedom from sexual stereotypes is the effect it may have on our children. Children need quality time with their parents. They need parents to be available when they hurt and when they celebrate their victories. They need the security of someone to come home to. Good day-care centers or baby sitters can fill the gap for short periods, but they are not adequate parent substitutes. When both parents—or single parents—have demanding careers, leaving them exhausted and distracted when they arrive home in the evening, the children suffer. Parents may feel too tired or too guilty to discipline the children. They may lack the emotional energy to listen carefully, to play or to spend special time with the children. Unless one or both parents readjust their priorities, major problems can develop.

We are free in Christ to be fully human—fully woman or fully man. The sexes are equal, and both are precious in God's sight. But we are not free to use that freedom for selfish gain, disregarding the needs and freedom of others. We are free to choose among many opportunities for our lifework without being limited by sexual stereotypes, but choose we must. The woman who chooses a demanding career may find that she must decide to be single, or at least childless, in order to do her job well. The superwoman who can do everything at once is a rare bundle of energy—or a myth. The man who chooses to spend more time in child rearing may have to sacrifice promotions or exciting

travel opportunities at work. H
odds with his employer's expec
be clear about our values and p
accordingly.

## Contentment and Change
Perhaps the key to understanding
women lies in Paul's statement ir
learned, in whatever state I am, t
things in him who strengthens m
between being content in our circ
dence that we can change the statu
Christ.

We can find contentment in bei
created each of us to be—male or
differences between men and womer
as helpmates, complementing one and
contentment with some of the injusti
perience, both in the church and in
them would take time and energy ne
tasks. We can also learn to be content
mitments we have made to employers,
church, community and others in need,
response to God's calling.

However, contentment is not apathy. T
change is mandatory, a time when we r
battle injustice, knowing that "I can do
strengthens me." For Melissa, that time c
her church continually told her she must s
physical abuse. For Phyllis, the time cam
church in a new community, she was told
permitted to study the Bible together since
al. Bob decided it was time for action wh
several of his graduate-assistant colleagu

grades of w
Wheneve
are being al
in the freed
a controve
criticism, re
tain our pe
sincerity o
ally, to ba
schism, or
overtones
tioned. T
women w
ened whe
be bathed
and wisd
God and
come fro

# 4
# Marriage, Singleness and God's Call

P HILOSOPHIZING OVER MALE and female roles in the church and society may produce stimulating conversation, but actually living those roles is another matter. The way men and women relate to one another has a direct bearing on how well they can fulfill God's calling. Men and women are created to complement and help one another (Gen 2:20-24). God created us with a natural mutual attraction and with a strong desire to be a part of a family. Problems set in when we do not bring those healthy and good desires into the broader sense of calling.

Jenny was headed for the mission field. Ever since attending a missionary convention during her sophomore year of college she had been convinced that God was calling her overseas. She applied to a mission board and began systematically meeting their requirements for missionaries. Then, in the last semester of her senior year, she met John.

John, though not a Christian, was enamored with Jenny's idealism and supportive of her goals. Jenny convinced herself that she and John were "just good friends," and she explained to people at the mission board that their relationship offered her good practice in relating to non-Christians. But by graduation time John had talked Jenny into waiting a year before going overseas. At the end of that year they were married.

After their wedding Jenny remained a committed Christian, and John maintained his skeptical respect for her faith. He did not prevent her from participating in Christian activities, but he did not join her either. Eventually Jenny realized that the more enthusiastic she became over her relationship with God and other Christians, the more distant she felt from John. She concluded that, practically speaking, she would have to choose between her marriage and her ministry. She withdrew from all Christian involvement except Sunday worship.

Jenny's situation is not unique. It is a common theme in the Scriptures, where we see Samson lured away from his calling by Delilah (Judg 16), David distracted by Bathsheba (2 Sam 11) and Solomon weakened by his marriages to foreign women (1 Kings 11). In the New Testament, Paul strongly warns, "Do not be mismated with unbelievers" (2 Cor 6:14). That is probably one of the most practical admonitions in the Scriptures. More Christian callings are thwarted by marriage to the wrong person than any other hindrance. Even another Christian may not be the ideal mate.

Jeff had a rewarding ministry with delinquent boys before his marriage. Each weekend he would bring two or three boys from a correctional institution home with him. They would go to sports events, educational programs and church activities together and spend hours just talking. Several of the boys became Christians. When Jeff married Susan, a strong Christian, he assumed that his ministry would continue and Susan would enjoy joining in. But Susan had different ideas. The boys frightened her, and she resented the time Jeff spent with them. Jeff was in a quandary. He felt called to work with the boys, but he also wanted to please Susan. He finally gave up his ministry.

The "urge to merge" commonly strikes college seniors with a vengeance. The prospect of facing the real world alone is frightening. Everybody else seems to be getting married. The realization suddenly strikes that the pool of available potential mates will never be this large again. Panic sets in. In my own college class, within a year after graduation only four of us remained unmarried. (The number still married to the same spouse grows smaller each year, however.) Another crisis period, when a similar desperation sets in, comes with the approach of age thirty. Both are times when Christians are most likely to let down their standards and marry the most convenient person.

About my sophomore year of college I began to see the problems which developed for my Christian friends when they married non-Christians or Christians with whom they had little in common. Once vital and active in their churches, they often became uninterested in and cut off from Christian activities. They were frequently consumed by guilt, anger and frustration. Our Nurses Christian Fellowship group also became concerned, and we began to study biblical principles for marriage. As a result, the president of the group ended her engagement to a non-Christian, and we all suffered with her. By the time she graduated, she was engaged to a Christian man we all considered the pick of the crop. We rejoiced that her faithfulness had been rewarded—but also felt a little twinge of envy.

## A Checklist for Marriage

After months of personal and group Bible study and wrestling in prayer about the matter, I managed to construct a checklist of qualities for a husband which convinced my family and friends that I was headed for lonely spinsterhood. But the Lord assured me that I would neither be lonely nor have time to sit around

## *THE CHECKLIST*

### Personal Qualifications

Am I secure and growing in my relationship with God?
Do I know what God is calling me to do?
Am I content and fully enjoying life as a single person?
Have I learned to depend on God alone?

### Qualities of Potential Spouse

Does he put the Lord first (before me) in life?
Can I trust God to be at work in him, and him to respond in obedience?

### Qualities of Our Relationship

Would our ministries be enhanced or hindered if we were to marry?
Can we pray, study Scripture and share spiritual insights with one another?
Do we enjoy the same friends and have similar attitudes about hospitality?
Do we have the same degree of caring and respect for parents and siblings?
Do we have the same attitudes toward money and giving?
Do we share intellectual interests?
Do we enjoy similar recreational activities?
Do we both have the same desire to have children (or not)?
Do we really know what the other expects from a spouse?
Can we honestly meet one another's role expectations?

---

and spin. Isaiah 54 became my theme song.

As the pressure to marry lessened, I felt a new freedom to explore God's calling. The ten years between college graduation and marriage were full and productive. I had time to work with students, take courses and establish new friendships. I also had enough money to hop on a plane to visit a friend in distress or send a student to camp or attend a convention in another country. There were times of extreme difficulty and aloneness (in spite of a house full of roommates), when I learned to depend entirely on God. Although I would never want to relive some of those years, I am deeply grateful for each of those experiences.

During that time my marriage checklist constantly remained in the back of my mind. In fact, it became more firmly planted there. Not that I was going around checking off prospective mates—it simply gave me an objective way to consider whether marriage was part of God's call to me at that time. It freed me not to think about finding a husband all the time.

The first part of the checklist dealt with my own readiness and maturity. I knew that I needed to learn faithfulness and obedience to God and to discover what he was calling me to be and do. Whenever I felt a relationship pulling me away from commitments and responsibilities I believed were God-given, a red flag would go up in my mind. I also needed to learn contentment and to gain meaning in life from serving the Lord rather than from another person. Unless I could be completely happy as a single person, I knew I could never be content in marriage.

There were times when I began to waver on this point. Times of emotional upheaval, such as after a move or when I felt discouraged with my work or experienced tensions in a friendship, made the security of marriage—to anyone—look awfully appealing. But each time, usually with great distress, I became overwhelmingly aware that I would disobey God if I succumbed. In the process I learned vivid lessons about God's love and faithfulness. His presence became palpably real.

The remainder of the checklist centered on the character of a potential spouse and the nature of our relationship. At the very top of the list was that the Lord had to come first—even before me—in that person's life. That eliminated non-Christians as well as all the starry-eyed Christian men who wanted a wife to worship. It took me thirty years to meet a man who met this qualification. There seemed to be plenty of terrific Christian men who put the Lord first, but they were all married to someone else. Then I met Jim at seminary, and we quickly became best friends. Soon after our relationship began, however, he carefully explained that he was not interested in any romantic involvements while in seminary because the Lord had called him to the ministry and he had to concentrate on studying.

A bell went off in the back of my head. Here was the first man to get past point one on my checklist—but he did it by saying he wasn't interested in marriage! That ironic situation freed us to develop a delightful friendship without the immediate pressures of romantic involvement. We spent hours studying together; talking about ideas, goals and dreams; sharing friendships, meals and classes. We started a seminary prayer group and participated in a small-group Bible study. We worked with a church youth group. About a year later, Jim said, "We make a pretty good team ministry," and another bell went off in my head. It wasn't long before we were talking about marriage.

At the top of my list for qualities of the relationship was the requirement that marriage would enhance, not hinder, each of our ministries. In working with Jim I had begun to notice that we were more effective together than either of us was alone. We seemed to enable each other to use our God-given gifts and talents more fully. Now that we have been married eight years, that requirement has proven wise indeed. With Jim's encouragement and support, I have experienced the most productive years of my life, and Jim frequently tells me how important our relationship is to his ministry.

A related requirement is being able to trust God to work in and through a potential spouse—and being able to trust that person to respond in obedience. Can you see obvious spiritual growth in the person? Does he or she spend time alone in prayer and Bible study and apply it to daily life? Does he or she consistently seek the Lord's direction in making choices?

The way you answer these questions can make a big difference in your marriage. Learning to trust God in another person is always difficult. In a marriage it can be doubly hard, because your own future is tied up with your spouse's responses to God. Obviously the major areas of decision making, like whether God is calling you to the mission field or whether you should have children, will have to be jointly entrusted to the Lord. You will want to believe that you will both come to the same understanding of God's will. But there are also a myriad of daily interactions which involve trusting God in one another. When Jim began his first pastorate I was often tempted to tell him how to do things, based on my Nurses Christian Fellowship staff experience. He became increasingly annoyed with my "wise teacher" attitude and told me so. After that, I began to pray whenever I felt like giving advice. To my amazement, Jim would come out of his study soon afterward and say, "I just had some good insights into how to handle . . ." He would then tell me exactly what I had wanted to tell him—or he would have a completely different, and better, idea.

Another important spiritual quality to consider is whether you can pray, study Scripture and share spiritual insights with each other. During the dating phase of a relationship, this is best kept within a group context. One-to-one prayer and deep spiritual sharing can arouse sexual feelings which confuse and distract. In marriage, that leads to a beautiful union which Ephesians 5 and Genesis 2 describe as becoming "one flesh." But in a dating relationship, the passion can quickly overwhelm any spiritual intentions and become all-consuming.

A group situation not only protects against lust, but also provides an opportunity to learn from others in a nonthreatening setting. Christians from various backgrounds learn different approaches to prayer and Bible study and may have difficulty adjusting to new styles when a spouse becomes the teacher. Bob and Mary Lou were both committed Christians, but they came from different backgrounds. Mary Lou became a Christian through a campus fellowship group which used a casual, familiar style of conversational prayer. Bob grew up in a deeply religious family in a liturgical church tradition which used formal, written prayers. After they were married, both Bob and Mary Lou felt strongly that they should have daily devotions together, but each day it became a source of contention. Bob was offended by Mary Lou's prayers, believing they were disrespectful. Mary Lou told Bob that reading prayers out of a book was not really praying. Later, in a prayer group, Bob learned to enjoy a freer manner of talking with God, and Mary Lou gained an appreciation for the majesty of God which her "good buddy" approach did not include. A common prayer group experience before marriage could have spared Mary Lou and Bob a great deal of tension later.

## Practical Considerations

Beyond overtly spiritual characteristics, there are practical considerations that affect how well a couple will be able to fulfill God's calling. Friends, family and finances, as well as shared interests, goals and values, can determine whether a couple will function well as a team or spend most of their time and energy mending their relationship.

Unless marriage partners have grown up together or attended the same school or church, a major phase of adjustment will be getting to know each other's friends and forming friendships together. If your friends are part of your ministry, it is especially important that a potential spouse be able to enjoy those friends as well. Jim and I have both been enriched by each other's friends. We have learned a great deal about one another through them, as well. A deep sense of satisfaction and continuity comes from bringing each other into the circle of people who influenced and shaped us over a lifetime.

Related to friendship is your attitude toward hospitality. Home means many different things to people. Some see it as a quiet sanctuary, while others prefer a beehive of activity. While one person may enjoy large crowds, another will prefer to invite only a few close friends at a time. Do you want your home to be a retreat from a hectic ministry or the center of it? It is best for each to know before marriage what the other expects from a home. If you expect to use your living room as a student center and your prospective spouse envisions a quiet haven for writing devotional verse, you are laying a foundation for conflict.

Attitudes toward family are an equally important consideration. Do you fit comfortably into each other's families? How often do you expect to see them after marriage? How will you handle major illness and disability of family members? Do you plan for your ill or widowed parents and in-laws to move into your home, and will you expect your spouse to care for them? Does he or she expect that of you? Marriage usually comes when young people are establishing independence from parents, so these questions may seem irrelevant and even morbid. But families are a part of our identities, and we usually have strong feelings when a crisis forces us to make choices. It is better to discuss attitudes and expectations before your widowed mother-in-law has a stroke and your spouse insists on providing her with twenty-four-hour care in the living room of your one-bedroom apartment.

Money is another major point of conflict in marriage. Attitudes toward spending, saving and giving are crucial areas that need to be discussed before marriage. Giving can be an especially touchy area if expectations are not made clear before marriage. Barbara discovered after her marriage to George that he would not give to any Christian work outside their denomination. Barbara was committed to supporting an old friend who was a missionary with an independent mission board. One day she confessed to me, "I feel so guilty, but the only way I can give to Joy's ministry is to sneak money out of the grocery budget."

Shared intellectual interests and recreational activities contribute to building a marriage which will also be a lasting friendship. It is important to be able to discuss subjects which are a bit more stimulating than what the dog did today or how long the kitchen faucet has been dripping. Do you both enjoy music, art, travel, sledding, archeology or bird watching? Do you enjoy doing activities together which expand your knowledge and stimulate your thinking or strengthen your muscles and stimulate your heart? Do you have similar desire for continuing education? What will you have in common with one another once the warm glow of infatuation wears off?

Role expectations in marriage also need to be discussed, not assumed. Larry and Chris worked together as colleagues before their marriage. One of the primary attractions Chris found in Larry was the way the two of them functioned as a team at work. After they were married, the nature of their relationship changed drastically. Larry became dominating and authoritarian, expecting Chris to stay at home and be subservient. Confused, Chris asked him why his behavior had changed. Larry replied, "You're a wife now, not a colleague."

Role expectations should include attitudes toward jobs. Should both husband and wife work? Whose job would take priority if a move were considered? Is the wife's job just a temporary position, or is she headed toward a career? Who will do the cooking, cleaning, laundry and dishes? How involved do you expect to be in each other's jobs? Will you expect your spouse to attend work-related parties and official functions? Will you want to entertain colleagues at home? How will you handle the preparation and clean-up for home entertaining?

Greg, a pastor, felt that the best way to get to know his church leaders was over a meal in his home. He also believed that the pastor's home should be a model for the congregation, so he encouraged members to drop by frequently. His wife, Beth, agreed with him in principle, but was teaching full-time and going to graduate school two nights a week. She felt overwhelmed by the added burden of entertaining. Greg realized her dilemma and agreed to do all the cooking and help with the dishes.

The number and spacing of children, and who will care for them, are also important areas for discussion and agreement. When Harry and Connie were married, Connie knew that Harry did not want children, but she assumed he would eventually change his mind. Harry remained firm in his resolve, and Connie's anger and resentment finally drove a wedge so deep that their marriage ended in divorce.

Joe and Nancy both wanted children, but had widely differing views of who would care for them. Joe assumed that Nancy would quit her job and stay home with the children. Nancy planned to continue working and expected Joe to share equally in child care. She assumed that the children would go to a day-care center while they were at work. They did not discover one another's views until Nancy was pregnant with their first child. Nancy prevailed with her part of the plan, but Joe constantly accused her of being a bad mother. He did not help with child care. They were divorced after their second child arrived.

During the warm glow of courtship so many of these questions seem like irrelevant details which can be resolved later, but they cut to the very core of our being. The way you and your prospective spouse answer the questions will determine whether or not you can marry each other and still be the person God has called you to be and do those things he has called you to do. Each of these issues should be settled before you announce your engagement. The growing sexual attraction and the pressure of friends and family make it extremely difficult to change your mind once the wedding date is set, the church reserved and the invitations mailed.

More and more Christian marriages are ending in divorce. Many that haven't are stormy at best. Christians are not immune to the pressures, attitudes and values of secular society. Although constant ridicule for maintaining your standards for a marriage partner may come from family and friends, causing you to question their validity, keep in mind that most of those who laughed loudest at my checklist are now divorced. Too many marriages—Christian marriages—are made for the wrong reasons: peer pressure, parental pressure, fear of being alone, sexual desire. Sometimes those marriages flourish, despite the odds, but most do not. They become a great millstone around the necks of God's servants, preventing them from serving him to the fullest.

## The Call to Singleness

Marriage is a calling, but God does not call each of us to the same task. For some the calling to remain single is an important alternative. In 1 Corinthians 7, the apostle Paul presents singleness as a higher calling because it allows a person to focus on the Lord's work rather than on mundane concerns. Remaining single is not second-best; it can be a clear choice.

Janice was an associate professor at a university. She took her job as a teacher seriously, putting extra time into her lecture preparation and giving special attention to each student who needed help. She was also an adviser to a campus fellowship group and spent her free time helping the group leaders and counseling Christian students. She had no time left over even for dating, much less being a wife. She knew God had called her to teaching and ministry with students. Her life was full as a single person.

Norman was a Navy chaplain. His job required him to move frequently and to spend months at sea each year. He was completely absorbed in his work and believed that he had a vital ministry, but realized that it would be incompatible with marriage. He also chose to remain single.

Singleness is a gift, and not everyone has that gift. However, some Christians refuse to accept the gift when God offers it. Ann was 27 and single, but consumed with a desire to be married. She

*JOB*

For many mothers the situation will be reversed. By
ght they will be sending their children off to college
o begin a new career. In either case, there comes a
one aspect of our calling is complete and God leads
ther dimension of his purpose for our lives.

our case it seems right to view my husband's call to
y as our family's primary calling. That does not di-
overall sense of calling to be a family, nor does it
my own work is less important. At times my work
nts take priority in our scheduling, but in general Jim's
our agenda, determines where we live and provides
ur interpersonal relationships. Logistically speaking,
s not enough time nor energy to juggle two separate
llings in one family.

hristian families have been able to balance two de-
areers with child rearing and have found it challenging
ing. Most of these people have high energy levels and
eal of discipline. However, what is possible for one
y not work for another. We have a responsibility to
ssess our gifts, values and personalities to determine
ve can provide adequate nurture for our families when
nts are career oriented. Nurturing a family is a high
nich usually (but not always and not exclusively) falls
e. Far from being a waste of gifts, talents and education,
s every bit of expertise and experience a person holds.
ars of intense nurturing can also provide opportunities
ve development and application of skills which may
your value in the work force. I don't think I would ever
ted writing books if Jim and I had not decided that I
rastically reduce my traveling and speaking engagements
to conserve energy for nurturing our marriage and fam-

hristians, marriage and family are integral parts of our
, not just a sideline. If we choose to be married and to

spent most of her waking hours trying to figure out how to find
a husband. She belonged to singles groups in three different
churches, went to a Christian singles camp each summer, took
courses at a local seminary and even tried a Christian computer-
dating service. She dated frequently, but men seldom called her
for a second date. Her desperation frightened them. In the meantime, Ann lost sight of what the Lord may have been calling her
to be and do.

The gift of singleness can be temporary, eventually replaced
with the gift of marriage, or it can be a lifelong calling. Accepting
the gift of singleness does not doom you to a lonely old age. Even
in singleness we are called to partnership with other Christians.
We are part of God's family. The Lord provides us with rich
friendships and loving care when we need it. He has promised
not to leave us desolate (Jn 14:18; Is 54:5-8). Married or single,
we are precious in his sight (Is 43:4) and called to live to the
praise of his glory (Eph 1:12).

### Nurturing Is Important

Current trends in our society show that we are in a transitional
period for sexual roles. The number of women entering the job
market is increasing by leaps and bounds. The number of women
who earn more than their husbands is slowly increasing. Single-
parent families are becoming more and more common. The "traditional family," where Dad goes to work while Mom stays home
to take care of 2.3 children, a dog and a cat, is becoming rare.
For some, especially women, these trends have been positive and
liberating. But for many women they have produced gnawing
guilt, frustration and anxiety.

The rush of women to the work force has not produced a
corresponding movement of men deciding to stay home with the
children. Although men sometimes share in the housework and
child care in two-career families, their wives usually bear the
greater portion of the work. More and more children are reared

in day-care centers (many of them quite good) and have little time with their parents. When these children become too old for day-care centers, they are often forced to come home from school to an empty house.

Christians are not immune to the prevailing trends and values in our culture. We frame them in evangelical lingo and claim them as our own. "Using my gifts to the fullest" may mean leaving the children with a baby sitter to go to work. "Recognizing my worth in God's sight" can become an excuse for a selfish disregard for the needs of others. There are times when it is necessary to arrange for child care in order to go to work, and there are many Christians with shattered self-esteem who need to learn to assert themselves; however, we must examine our motivation before blindly following the crowd.

Families need time, attention and nurturing to be stable and satisfying. Too many Christians see their roles as husband, wife and parent as avocations rather than part of their primary calling. We have become convinced by the world around us that we can do everything at once, and do it well—until we try it. I know that I cannot work forty hours a week, keep the house clean, provide nutritious meals, emotionally support and encourage my husband and be an attentive mother—even with Jim sharing almost equally in the cleaning and child care. The thirty hours I used to spend on the job became more difficult as our daughter blossomed into a toddler. She used to sleep contentedly in her playpen while I typed. Now she wants to sit in my lap and type with me. She races me for the phone when it rings. Her younger brother will have nothing to do with playpens. As their needs have increased, my working hours have had to decrease. We have made a choice to be parents and, for now, that commitment overrides other aspects of our calling.

I have wrestled with the *whys.* Why should I cut back, and not my husband? Why not find a baby sitter or day-care center? Why not work in shifts, doing my work when Jim is available to watch

the children? The Scriptures d
prophetess and judge Deborah
his men, apparently leaving he
at home (Judg 4:4—5:31). We
of the women who followed J
mother of James). Although Titu
be "domestic" and "submissive
3:4, 12 says that male church le
dren and households well. Home
responsibilities. Certainly, the "e
ogists, psychiatrists and other co
answer. Each authority seems to l
is best for family dynamics. I can d
and a prayerful seeking for direc
not be appropriate for all other f
ciples do apply to decision makii
fork in the road of their calling.

First of all, it seems very natural t
right now. I enjoy spending time w
to be available when they need me
conversations to be boring and su
care about was their children's dev
I become ecstatic over each new wo
to visibly foster each child's self-es
in a day-care center.

Second, I am feeling a sense of cc
career. My work has been strongly i
was a God-given vision. The fulfill
within sight. I have had a strong sen
me to stimulate and enable others
spiritual care of patients, not to set m
the subject. That has happened, so I ca
the fruit of my labors. The fact that Jai
eighth birthday allowed me the time

completion.
age thirty-ei
and ready t
time when
us into ano

Finally, i
the ministr
minish our
mean that
commitme
work sets
most of o
there just
primary ca

Some C
manding c
and satisfy
a great de
family ma
carefully a
whether v
both pare
calling wl
to the wit
it require
Those ye
for creati
enhance
have star
should d
in order
ily.

For C
vocation

have children, then we must take seriously the responsibilities that go with those choices. For men and women who feel called to a demanding career, that leaves several options.

The first option is to remain single. A single person is freer to expend his or her nurturing energy on the job. The helping professions, especially, require an enormous output of the same emotional energy needed for supporting a spouse and children. A single person who has dealt with needy people all day will not usually have to come home to another set of people demanding attention and support.

A second option is to cut back on work commitments while remaining in your chosen career. This option may reduce your opportunities for advancement, but it can simplify your life. Refusing overtime and out-of-town travel, turning down most after-hours socializing with colleagues, or taking a less prestigious but less demanding job can provide more family time.

Another option is to postpone career goals until your children are older. This is not as difficult or as disadvantageous as it sounds. Second careers are becoming more common for both men and women. Usually by the time a person reaches the late thirties he or she begins to re-evaluate career achievements and goals and may make a radical change in occupation. Taking a refresher course in your original job skills, going back to college for another degree, or building on more recently acquired skills and interests may lead you into a satisfying new career in midlife.

Choosing is often difficult, even painful and frightening; but not choosing responsibly can lead us into a rat race of guilt, frustration and anxiety. In the end, we may not do a good job of fulfilling any aspect of our calling in life. By prayerfully making wise choices we can enjoy the fullness of God's calling in our lifework.

# 5
# Survival Skills
# for Working People

O NLY THE DEVIL IS in a hurry; the Lord has eternity on his hands." The pastor's words struck me head-on. I was listening to the sermon with one ear, while writing my "to do" list for the week. Doing two or more things at once was becoming more than a habit at this stage of my life; it was a compulsion. I was working sixty to eighty hours a week, struggling with some touchy interpersonal relationships and trying to maintain an active social life on the side. The hectic pace was beginning to take its toll. The harder I worked, the less I seemed to accomplish. Physical and emotional exhaustion finally set off a thyroid condition which forced me to pull back and re-evaluate what I was doing and why.

In contrast to my own feverish activity, I began to notice that Jesus was never in a hurry. If anyone had a right to feel hassled, Jesus did. First of all, his job description was seemingly impossible. He was the only person ever called to save the whole world. His daily schedule was horrendous. Matthew 4:23-25 tells us: "He went about all Galilee, teaching in their synagogues and preaching the gospel of the kingdom and healing every disease and every infirmity among the people. So his fame spread throughout all Syria, and they brought him all the sick, those afflicted with various diseases and pains, demoniacs, epileptics, and paralytics, and he healed them. And great crowds followed him. . . ." Now that is pressure.

But Jesus did not succumb to the pressures and expectations of the crowds. He knew how to set limits (Mt 8:19), how to get away to spend time with his heavenly Father (Mk 1:35-39) and how to delegate responsibility (Mt 9:35—10:1). He faced ridicule (Mt 9:24), false accusations (9:34) and fierce opposition (12:14) with confidence, remaining undistracted from his calling (12:15-16). His clear priorities also gave him the ability to remain calm under pressure from his family (Mt 12:46-50). Jesus, though deeply compassionate and sensitive to people's needs, never seemed controlled by the neediness around him. Constantly keeping sight of his ultimate calling, he was able to say no when necessary and to withdraw from the crowds, despite their demands, when he needed spiritual refreshment. He laid down his life for his "sheep" (Jn 10:15), but he never talked about "burning out for the Lord." After three short years of ministry he could say from the cross, "It is finished" (Jn 19:30).

Can an ordinary Christian have as clear a picture of God's calling as Jesus did? Perhaps not, but the Scriptures provide some fairly clear guidelines for our use of time and priority setting. We have already established that our primary calling is to "live for the praise of his glory" (Eph 1:12). Within the context of that calling we can discover some priorities for our time.

Romans 13:11-14 describes the importance of godly behavior as a way to avoid wasting time. At first that seems like a strange connection, but consider the time and emotional energy we expend feeling guilty over past sins. This paralyzes us and keeps us from moving ahead. Petty bickering and jealousy can keep us from working together effectively with other Christians. Self-righteousness and insensitivity can quickly thwart our attempts to communicate the gospel to non-Christians. Our own sinfulness is a terrible time waster. According to 2 Corinthians 3:18, the way to overcome sin in our lives is to turn to the Lord and allow him to change us. Time in prayer, meditation and Bible study are top priorities in the Christian life.

The fifth chapter of Ephesians reinforces the idea that careful attention to behavior is a way to make the most of time (vv. 15-17). The chapter then adds another dimension: our relationships with other Christians, including those within the family, must also be a priority (5:21—6:4). Colossians 3:12-17 adds further details about Christian priorities. We are to encourage and support one another in the work of the gospel, to maintain a spirit of joy and thankfulness, and to come together in an atmosphere of love, forgiveness and harmony. We need each other in order to be effective in our calling. The free-lance Christian, who attempts to live and work apart from the body, may start out in a blaze of glory but end up defeated and discouraged. Christian fellowship is a high priority in our lives.

We must also make the most of time in our evangelism efforts. Colossians 4:5-6 tells us: "Conduct yourselves wisely toward outsiders, making the most of the time. Let your speech always be gracious, seasoned with salt, so that you may know how you ought to answer every one." Here we are told to behave "wisely" toward non-Christians. That includes knowing when not to witness as well as when to speak up. It means being honest and fair with an employer's time and equipment (like not using the word processor and work time to make copies of songs for your church youth group). We are to be careful about what we say and how we say it. We are to speak graciously, not condemning or acting self-righteous. Seasoning our words with salt includes wit and humor as well as affirmation, for salt is both a flavoring and a preservative.

It is interesting that we are to "know how to answer every one," not have a speech ready to give whenever we feel like witnessing. We are expected to listen to the questions, then to answer appropriately. That requires a lot more preparation than a canned presentation of the gospel (although it is handy to have an outline of the gospel memorized with corresponding Scripture passages). At times we may have to say, "I don't know the answer, but I'll find out and get back to you." Not only have we then admitted that we are human, but we may have opened the door for further conversation about spiritual things or even to an investigative Bible study.

So the Scriptures give us three major priorities in our lives: (1) our personal relationship with God; (2) our relationships with other believers, including our family members; and (3) our relationships with non-Christians. With these major priorities in mind, we can begin to focus on our specific calling and how we should plan our time and energy.

### Determining Present Priorities

Do you know what your present goals are? Perhaps they are very concrete at this time: to finish school, to get a job, to find a spouse, or even just to pass the next test. Those are short-term goals, and they need to be subordinated to an overall set of long-term purposes. Why do you want to finish school? How will your job fit into your ministry as a Christian? What are you looking for in a mate? What difference would it make, in terms of eternity, if you failed the test?

An exercise I frequently use when speaking to groups about time management has proved revealing. First, I ask people to write down their purpose in life in one sentence. Next, I hand them a blank chart with a week divided into days and hours and ask them to fill in how they spent the previous week. You would expect the distribution of time to reflect the stated purpose in life, but most are appalled at the lack of correspondence between goals set and time spent. Before you sit back and feel smug, try it yourself. Let's say you manage to squeeze in fifteen minutes of quiet time each weekday morning, spend thirty minutes preparing your Sunday-school lesson, go to Sunday school and Sunday morning worship, and attend a weekly Bible study. You also watch an hour of TV news five days a week and about six hours of other programming. Already you have spent almost twice as much time in front of the television as you spent in spiritual refreshment and Christian fellowship. You may also be amazed at how much time you simply can't account for. You know you lived through Thursday, but except for going to work and coming home the day draws a blank in your mind. At the same time, you may have been convincing yourself that you have been too busy to answer the stack of mail on your desk or to spend an extended time in prayer and Bible study or to visit a sick friend.

Charting your use of time can be painful, because it confronts you with your real goals in life. We may earnestly believe that our purpose in life is "to glorify God and enjoy him forever," but when concrete evidence of evangelism, spiritual growth and fellowship with God and his people is clearly lacking, we begin to realize that our unconscious goals are to be comfortable and avoid anxiety.

Of course, a time chart does not tell the whole story. Time at work can be used for a ministry of evangelism, comfort and encouragement, or it can be just a job. Time in front of the television can serve to educate us to the needs and concerns of the world, or it can be an escape from the world. Fellowship with other Christians can equip us to go out into secular society with the good news of the gospel, or it can be a cozy cocoon to insulate us from non-Christians. Even extended time in prayer, if not practiced with a spirit of humility and openness to God, can be merely self-righteous prattling (see Mt 6:5-15; Lk 18:9-14).

A good way to use a completed time chart is as a basis for prayer. First, confess the inconsistencies between what you believe is God's will for your life and how you actually spent the time he entrusted to you last week. Then think about what went wrong and why. Perhaps that lost Thursday was a bad day at work. For instance, your supervisor gave you an unreasonable assignment and you seethed over it all day. In turn, you snapped at your colleagues and clients. By the time you got home you had no energy left over for any constructive activity, so you turned on the TV and sat on the sofa watching whatever came on the screen until midnight. In this case, the problem was not the TV, but your attitude and behavior at work. You could ask God to help you "conduct yourself wisely" at work so the same problem won't develop again.

Next, make a chart for the week ahead, prayerfully planning how you will spend each day. Try to be realistic—everybody needs some blank space. The schedule should be tight enough to accomplish those things which need to be done, but loose enough to allow flexibility for unplanned interruptions.

### Identifying Time Wasters
Wasting time is seldom a conscious choice. Nor is it usually done by just sitting around doing nothing. Wasted time can be filled with frantic activity. On the other hand, time well spent can be a serendipitous moment which was totally unplanned. What makes the difference? Basically, it comes down to whether or not we are doing what God has called us to do.

A lack of clear priorities can dissipate time and energy in a hurry. We get caught up in the "tyranny of the urgent"[7] and allow the good to crowd out God's best in our lives. For example, when a friend calls and suggests taking a class with her, you agree even though you are only slightly interested in the subject. Or your supervisor asks you to work a double shift, and you can't think of anything better to do with your evenings, so you agree. Or it's

Saturday, and rather than staying home alone you go shopping, even though you don't need anything.

A person with clear priorities seldom has time to be bored and rarely accepts a commitment without evaluating it against those priorities. If you have already considered your continuing education needs, it is much easier to tell your friend, "I'm really not interested in that course, but let me check the catalog and see if I need another one on the same evening—we could still ride together."

Closely related to a lack of priorities is the inability to say no. A request for help or the offer of a responsible position in an organization or church can be a real ego booster. It makes us feel needed and important. Saying no makes most people feel guilty, especially if the request comes in person or over the phone. I have worked hard at learning to say no graciously—and I have to do it frequently—but I still feel guilty when I do. However, I feel even worse when I say yes to something that creates a conflict with my priorities.

Last week my husband came home from a local ministerial meeting with a beautiful example of the results of saying no. The seminary professor scheduled to give an exposition of the Gospel of Matthew cancelled at the last minute—to go to his daughter's violin recital. One of the pastors in the group volunteered to speak on the same topic. "It was one of our best meetings," Jim reported. Not only was the talk much more practical than it might have been with the professor's more academic approach, but the professor communicated to a group of workaholic pastors that it is okay to put your family's needs first at times, even if it means disappointing your audience.

But even as this professor was a good example of saying no, he was probably guilty of another major time waster—poor planning. Poor planning takes many forms. For instance, Jane routinely schedules two things at once and then spends hours on the phone rearranging her schedule. Ron schedules appointments too close together, so he is always late and ends up wasting other people's time. Mark doesn't plan at all, and that leads to even more wasted time. I have found that I even need to schedule my free time, especially time alone with the Lord. Although I am a precise planner on workdays, on days off my efficiency falls apart. All I have to do is sleep until it is time for the children to get up, and quiet time will get lost in the bustle of family activities.

A more subtle time waster is the failure to delegate. The "I'll take care of it" syndrome looks like a time saver at first glance. I fell into this pattern too often as a staff nurse. I'd be giving medications when a patient's light would come on. Since I was close by, I would go in to check on the patient and find him in need of cleaning up and a linen change. Instead of calling the nurse's aide to help, I would go ahead and do the messy job myself. As a result, I would be late distributing the rest of the medications, and the aide would spend half the shift in the ladies' room, smoking.

Even though a failure to delegate may come from the best motives ("I don't want to push the dirty work onto someone else"; "I don't want to burden another person"), it may communicate a negative message. A committee member who is never asked to do anything may conclude that the chairperson thinks she is incompetent. When two or three people do most of the work in a church, other members may feel left out. The long-term effects of failing to delegate can be terribly wasteful. When the person who has been doing all the work finally quits, no one else is prepared to continue the job.

Poor communication is another time waster. You ask someone to do a project, but hesitate to give many instructions because it might seem pushy. The person is not really sure what you want, but he doesn't want to appear foolish, so he asks no questions. The completed project doesn't come close to what you need. You have now entered a cycle of poor communication, because you don't want to offend the person by saying his work is all wrong.

A pattern of poor communication once set off a dangerous situation in a hospital where I worked. When newly graduated nurses began orientation, older nurses would respond to their questions by saying, "You mean they didn't teach you that in school?" After a while, the younger nurses stopped asking questions. One evening, a nurse who had been working for about six months frantically called me to help her with a procedure which wasn't working. I discovered she was doing it backward, which could have caused pain and serious complications. Finally, she admitted she had never done the procedure before. When I asked why she didn't tell me when I assigned it to her, she said, "I didn't want to look stupid."

Inefficiency can also consume valuable time. Writing appointments on a central calendar is more efficient than tacking a dozen notes on the refrigerator door. Using carbon paper to type four sets of directions takes less time than driving five miles to the nearest photocopy machine. Categorizing mail as it arrives rather than tossing it all in a pile on the desk saves handling it twice. But inefficiency is tempting because it seems like a time saver at the moment. Getting organized requires an initial time investment in order to save time in the end.

Indecisiveness and procrastination also waste time—usually someone else's. Have you ever called a workshop registrar the day after the deadline for registration to ask if you may still come? The kindhearted registrar says, "Of course you may still come," and then has to make three phone calls and two trips across the building to arrange for your presence. The next day, when your best friend decides to go too, the friendly registrar (who can't say no) begins her rounds again.

Postponing decision making can waste your own time. Bob could never decide on a topic for his term papers until the last minute. When he finally started his review of the literature, none of the books he needed were still in the library. Marcia could not decide on a major until well into her junior year of college, so she had to spend an extra year in school. George could not decide between two good job offers. By the time he made his decision, the jobs had gone to other applicants.

## Building on Your Personal Style

Planning, communication and decisiveness can help us structure our time. Efficiency helps us get more things done in the time available. Delegation shares the workload, multiplying a leader's output. But human beings are not machines, so we must also consider the human element in managing time. One person's time-management scheme may be another person's undoing. The key to fulfilling God's purposes for your life is to discover how you, as an individual, function best.

For years I felt like a second-class Christian because I was not a morning person. So many of the spiritual giants I read about and observed extolled the virtue of rising early to spend hours on their knees. Every time I tried it, I fell asleep and spent the rest of the day feeling exhausted. But I could spend joyous hours in prayer and Bible study in the afternoon and evening. Somehow that didn't seem as virtuous, though. When I worked the 7—3 shift, my eyes never opened until eight o'clock, and I went home and collapsed after work. But when I worked 3—11, I was energetic at work yet still had plenty of energy left over to do other things the rest of the day. After I began to accept myself as an afternoon and evening person and to plan my schedule accordingly, I was amazed at how much more productive I could be.

Other considerations for planning your most effective use of time include how you work with other people, the nature of your work setting, and whether pressure motivates or discourages you. Extroverts tend to be energized by crowds. Introverts usually are emotionally drained by them. People with a gift for administration can see the needs of groups of people without being distracted by individual problems, whereas people with counseling gifts can focus intensely on the concerns of one person.

Our personalities and the way we relate to other people are dimensions of the gifts God gives us. It is important to allow ourselves, and one another, to be the people God created us to be. For instance, one person may enjoy making phone calls while another dreads it so much that it takes her thirty minutes just to work up the courage to dial. On the other hand, the person who hates making phone calls may effortlessly write beautiful letters, while the friendly caller may become cold and abrupt in writing. By considering the emotional energy involved in a task, we can plan our time more effectively. For example, I have discovered that speaking at a workshop usually takes about two weeks out of my writing time. The week before goes toward preparation, and the week after to recharging my emotional batteries. I now keep my speaking engagements to a minimum, because I believe that God has called me primarily to write.

The nature of your work setting may have a similar influence on your use of time. Some people need the discipline of going to work at a certain time each day, punching the time clock at the beginning and end of the day. Clear job descriptions and predictable structure free them to work effectively. Others feel stifled in such a setting, working better in an unstructured environment with only a long-term vision to provide direction and motivation for personally constructed short-term goals. Fitting your work setting to your personality will enable you to make the most of time. For instance, Polly found herself just going through the motions of staff nursing without much enthusiasm. She decided to go back to school to gain certification as a nurse practitioner. The stimulation of being her own boss and setting her own schedule and the variety she encountered in her new role gave Polly fresh excitement about her job. Craig, on the other hand, seemed to be working all the time but accomplishing little in his unstructured job as a campus staff worker. After switching to accounting, he finally felt in control of his time, since he had a visible way of measuring accomplishment.

Deadlines and pressure do not have the same effect on everyone. For some, deadlines stimulate action. For others, pressure brings on an immense paralysis. Ann, who always crumbled under pressure at school, became a dynamic youth worker because her relaxed pace made her easily available to the teen-agers and able to hear and respond to their concerns. But Les, a reporter, saw pressure as a challenge. He took great pride in that his stories not only met the deadlines, but were finished early.

Probably one of the biggest time wasters is trying to live by our perception of other people's expectations. Rather than functioning according to our own personalities, interests and talents, we do what we think other people want us to do. Mike, an excellent teacher who loved his students, became a mediocre and unhappy lawyer because he assumed that his father expected him to carry on the family tradition. Phil, a rock musician with a tremendous ministry to his audiences and other musicians, stopped playing in his band and became a factory worker because he was afraid the people in his church did not approve of rock music. Melody, a grade-school teacher with two young children, stopped teaching because she feared being considered a "bad mother" for working.

The advice and encouragement of people who know us well can be one way God directs us, but it should not control us. Mike, Phil and Melody went one step further: they allowed themselves to be controlled, not by reasoned advice but by what they thought other people were thinking. A person who fears disapproval may find opportunities for ministry severely limited. Jesus was constantly criticized (Mt 11:19; Lk 4:23; Jn 11:32); so was the apostle Paul (2 Cor 2:1-4). If we allow the fear of criticism to determine our decisions, crowding out the call of God, we are wasting our time.

## Making the Most of Time

Tom was frustrated. "I was flunking out of college, so I took a course on goal setting and time management. I organized my life and started working toward specific goals. I ended up with straight A's—and an ulcer." All the tricks of time management are useless if they merely push us into a stressful, success-oriented lifestyle. The purpose of planning should be to free us to answer God's call, not to tie us up in knots.

The first thing to keep in mind when setting goals is God's overall purpose for our lives. We have already determined that God puts top priority on relationships. The Christian perspective on relationships is a bit different from that of the business world. We are not to develop relationships in order to use people, but to serve them. There are priorities in Christian relationships. First comes our relationship with God (Mt 22:37-39). That comes before any human relationships, yet it enhances every other relationship. Second are our family relationships. We are to honor our parents (Ex 20:12), but after marriage, our spouse becomes a more primary commitment (Eph 5:31). Children come next, then relationships within the church, at work, and to the community and the world at large (Eph 6:1-4; Jn 13:34-35; 17:20-23).

Keeping godly priorities in mind makes planning and decision making easier. For example, when family relationships are constantly strained by one or both of the parents' church involvement, it is time to consider how commitments can be reduced. When job pressures prevent you from worshiping and serving in the church, you may need to reduce your workload or rearrange your schedule, even if it threatens your advancement. The decisions may be painful, but God's priorities must be observed at the beginning of the planning process.

Next, in the light of your priorities, consider what God has specifically called you to do, then break your overall goal down into measurable short-term goals. Work goals will be determined by your job description. For personal goals it may be helpful for you to think in terms of physical, psychosocial and spiritual objectives. Physically, we need to take good care of our bodies in

## *AREAS TO CONSIDER WHEN SETTING PERSONAL GOALS*

---

**Physical**
Weight/diet
Grooming
Sleep
Exercise
Routine health care

---

**Psychosocial**
Supportive relationships (including family)
Socialization
Hobbies
Cultural enrichment
Continuing education
Professional growth
Community service
Relaxation/recreation

---

**Spiritual**
Personal prayer and Bible study
Prayer partner/family devotions
Small group fellowship
Church affiliation/involvement
Giving (time, talent, money)
Evangelism (praying for a non-Christian, starting a Bible study at work, etc.)
Missions (short-term, supporting or corresponding with a missionary, praying)
Opportunities for spiritual growth (workshops, conferences, camps, etc.)

---

order to serve God with them. That means setting goals for proper rest, exercise, diet, and medical and dental care. Psychosocially, we need to set goals which will promote optimal emotional health and intellectual growth. This involves planning recreation, family time, cultural input and continuing education, including reading and television viewing. It is also helpful to set goals for friendships you want to cultivate, planning times to be together. Spiritual goals should include time for personal devotions and extended prayer and Bible study, as well as the time you wish to spend on church involvement, work with parachurch organizations, Bible studies, prayer groups, family devotions, evangelism and opportunities for Christian growth and service (camps, conferences, mission projects and so on).

Goals should be specific so that you can measure whether they have been met. For instance, a goal to jog one mile five days a week is easy to measure, but a goal to "get enough exercise" is too vague. "Spend time together as a family" sounds admirable, but "reserve Tuesday from six to eight for games with children" is more likely to be remembered.

If you believe God is calling you to a ministry which will require specific education and experience, you may need to construct a five- or ten-year plan. Let's say that you want to be a missionary. First you'll need to contact a mission board to discover their requirements, and then you'll need to systematically plan to meet them. For instance, you may need a graduate degree in your field and a year of Bible school, five years' experience in your profession, plus evidence of your ability to serve as a volunteer in various church or parachurch roles (not unusual for countries which will not grant a visa unless they think you will be an asset to their country). You'll need to determine where you can gain the type of work experience that will be most useful on the field, begin applying to schools, and carefully structure your courses to prepare you for what lies ahead. In the meantime, try to find Christian organizations in your vicinity which have similar ministries in this country as your mission board has abroad. Volunteer to help them. It will sharpen your ministry skills and give you practice working with other Christians. The experience may also refocus your vision.

When I graduated from college, I was sure God was calling me to India to do student work. The mission board I talked with recommended a plan similar to what I just outlined. After four years in two different nursing jobs and working with Nurses Christian Fellowship as an associate staff member, I joined NCF staff full-time. It was not exactly India, but I strongly sensed God's leading. After four years on staff, I took off two years to go to seminary. It occurred to me that India could still be on the horizon, but I also felt a definite calling to develop materials to help nurses meet spiritual needs. My goals were so clearly set that every course I took fit in as part of the whole to equip me for the task I believed God was calling me to do. After graduation I went back to NCF to use my seminary training in writing and editing. I still have not gotten to India, but my books have, and I can feel that God has used me to minister there through them. We may get to India eventually, or we may not, but the discipline of preparing has equipped me for my ministry in a way that sitting back and getting stuck in a directionless rut could never have accomplished.

There is a delicate balance between careful planning and being open to God's intervention. There is a temptation to make an idol of our goals or to feel guilty and defeated if they don't work out. Planning is important, but we must hang onto our plans loosely, constantly giving them over to the Lord. He may want to change them.

Ecclesiastes tells us: "For everything there is a season, and a time for every matter under heaven" (Eccles 3:1). The seasons of our lives provide variety and refreshment. Jesus experienced a new season in his life when he switched careers from carpenter to teacher at age thirty. Paul interspersed seasons of travel with seasons of staying in one place training church leaders and making tents. John Mark took a season off from his missionary work, but then returned (Acts 15:37-39). Changing goals and direction is not necessarily a sign of weakness. Although the job-hopper, who never stays long enough to live with his mistakes, or the dabbler, who drifts in and out of activities without commitment, may be acting irresponsibly, there are times in our lives when change is healthy. We need to learn to recognize the signs of those times in order to move into a new season with expectancy.

## Changing Direction

One sign of a need for change is failure to thrive. For example, Joy believed God was calling her to be a counselor. After six years of preparation and five years of practice, she had become overwhelmed with her clients' problems. She had trouble setting limits and allowed clients to call as often as they wished. She brought their problems home with her. She had little time or energy left over for her family. In consultation with her own therapist, Joy finally decided that she needed to work with emotionally healthy people for a while. She went back to school and prepared to be a director of Christian education. Joy blossomed in her new role She was able to use her counseling skills in working with church youth and their parents, in many cases averting serious problems which would have sent the family into therapy.

Failure can be even more difficult to handle when it comes as a surprise. Renee thought she and Bob had a good marriage until the day he came home and announced he wanted a divorce. Howard held a responsible position in a company, but after twenty-one years his boss told him he was fired. Jack found a good job after college only to be laid off six months later. In each case, the person felt betrayed and worthless. Self-esteem plummeted. It was hard for these people to pick up the pieces of their lives and consider where God was leading them.

Without a supportive Christian community, failure can be devastating and lead to despair rather than creative change. But God can turn failure into a blessing. What looks like the end of hope can be the beginning of a fuller vision. Failure helps us mature, reveals our humanity, and helps us to identify with people who need our help. I've come to believe that failure is a prerequisite for effective Christian service, for it is only in our weakness that we can yield to God's strength (2 Cor 12:10).

Another sign of a new season is when God equips us with new gifts and interests. Sometimes the gifts and interests he gives us lead us into change that we may not understand for many years. My friend Ramona is a good example. She started her career as an English teacher, but a sense of dissatisfaction led her into nursing. She sampled several different types of nursing, gaining a wide but seemingly unrelated experience. Gradually she realized that God had given her a gift for meeting the spiritual needs of her patients, and her interests began to focus in that area. She thought God was leading her into a hospital chaplaincy, so she went to seminary. Instead, when she graduated from seminary and completed extra work in hospital chaplaincy, God brought together her apparently unrelated experiences to equip her for her present role as editor of the *Journal of Christian Nursing.*

God also uses changing circumstances to lead us into a new season. Marriage, divorce, death of a spouse, children born and children grown will change our priorities and commitments. Retirement from a job, changing health and changing financial status can lead us into new phases of ministry. For example, after her husband's death, with both her children grown, Betty joined her sister as a missionary in Japan. When Wayne retired from the Air Force with a generous pension, he and his wife moved across the country to volunteer their time in maintaining missionary airplanes and providing support services. Even the sudden tragedy of serious illness or disabilities can be used for God's glory. Joni Eareckson Tada, for instance, realized her potential for ministry only after becoming paralyzed. When we realize that God is sovereign, we can believe that he will use even the worst tragedy for good. Our part is to keep asking, "What is God doing here?" and ite live up to their ideal.

e groups may seem ideal because they are so homoge-
at they are "spiritual hothouses." Darryl and Marie settled
university town after graduate school. They continued to
Collegiate Memorial Church. The pastor was a nationally
speaker and author with a weekly radio program. The
gation was divided into neighborhood Bible studies which
ch week. The studies were always stimulating and well
d. An impressive missions program kept a steady flow of
ding speakers coming to the church for Sunday evening
s. The Sunday school had few children, but four of the
dult classes could be taken for college credit. Darryl was
er and Marie coordinated the children's Sunday-school

ten years as members of Collegiate Memorial Church,
came home from an elders meeting and told Marie that it
ne for a change. The elders had been discussing potential
in the church and came up with a list of two hundred
out of four hundred fifty members. As Darryl and Marie
they realized that not only was the church overstocked
aders, but most of the members were between 18 and 45,
college educated, and middle class. They were in a spir-
othouse. They decided to transfer to a struggling mission
closer to their home.

ing the hothouse for whatever reason can be a painful
ence. The average local church is much more heterogene-
an these spiritual hothouses. In an average church, perhaps
per cent of the members attended college. Most of those
not in a campus fellowship group. A Bible study with small
discussion may seem shocking and threatening to many
ers. Only a small minority have daily devotions. Most do
ad the Bible regularly. Many members would not dare to
up in a discussion group, but nevertheless have a deep,
faith which has brought them through the trials of life. Yet

"What is the obedient response in this situation?"

Throughout life we are faced with changing circumstances. The
job you so diligently prepared for in college may not be available
when you graduate. Opportunities today may be closed doors
tomorrow. God has called us to be faithful and to make the most
of the time. Careful planning, with a willingness to change those
plans if God so leads, will make us more effective servants in the
Lord's kingdom.

# 6
# Living and W
# in the Body o

**C**HRISTIAN FELLOWSHIP IS a key elemen
changing circumstances and to discern Go
can help us use our time and talents wise
give us survival skills for the working worl
is part of our calling from God. But findir
be a long, painful process, especially if you
expectations.

Most Christians have experienced som
which becomes for them the ideal. For so
local church they attended while going to
may be a campus fellowship group, Bible s
camp. This group may have been such a po
it becomes the standard against which all
measured. When they graduate from colleg
when they are faced with finding fellowshi

may qu
Thes
nous th
in their
attend
known
congre
met ea
attende
outstan
service
seven
an eld
classes
After
Darryl
was tir
leader
names
talked
with l
Anglo,
itual h
church
Lea
exper
ous th
fifteer
were
group
meml
not re
speak
stead

chances are they don't express that faith the way *you* do. Their values, background and lifestyles are different.

The church was never intended only to meet our needs for supportive friendships. Jesus established it to fulfill his command to "go . . . and make disciples of all nations, baptizing them in the name of the Father and of the Son and of the Holy Spirit, teaching them to observe all that I have commanded you" (Mt 28:19-20). That involves learning to love, work with, and empathize with people who are not just like you. It may mean learning about enduring faith from a seventy-year-old woman who never went beyond the sixth grade, or learning about love from a child with Down's syndrome, or learning to serve by tearing up old sheets to make bandages for mission hospitals. Church is part of our calling from God, and the church will help us to do God's will in everyday life and in our jobs.

## What to Look for in a Church

Some of our own needs should be met in a church. If your church offers no opportunities for spiritual growth, fellowship, or service, you probably should look elsewhere. If you are a relatively new Christian, with little doctrinal or biblical teaching, you may need to be in an "intensive care" church where there is lots of spiritual food with few demands. If you spend a great deal of your time during the week in ministry, you will need a church which can refuel you for the week ahead.

There have been periods in my life when I felt "burned out" and needed a church which could minister to me without making demands. However, I began to stagnate when I stayed too long in an intake mode. The church should provide us with a way of serving, as well as serving us. If all the gifted leaders and teachers concentrate in a few dynamic congregations, that leaves the majority of churches foundering.

One of the major things we need to consider in looking for a church is whether there are *opportunities to serve.* Perhaps you

have a gift for working with youth, and a church you are considering is desperate for a youth advisor. Or maybe you enjoy doing
manual labor on weekends, and a church in your community has
a work team which helps the elderly and handicapped to maintain their houses and property. Or you have just returned from
a short-term missions project abroad, and you find a church in
your new town where the pastor is trying to start a missions
committee to communicate a vision for missions to the congregation. You may be just the person with the gifts needed to build
up that part of the body.

The *qualities of the pastor* are an important consideration in
choosing a church, but you will want to look at the congregation
itself, as well. Pastors move. They may, or may not, reflect the
character of the congregation as a whole. There is no such thing
as a perfect pastor. An outstanding preacher may be a poor counselor. A strong motivater and encourager may stutter in the pulpit.
Some basic qualities, though, are important. The pastor should
teach sound doctrine and preach from the Scriptures, have a
vision for ministry, and be an example of godly living. You should
feel like you would be able to support him or her in times of
crisis or dissension. It helps if he is approachable and can understand your point of view, but that is not essential.

The *"personality" of the congregation* can be more important
than the qualities of the pastor. Some congregations seem to exist
to maintain the status quo in a community. That's not all bad. In
our transient society, it is nice to find some stability, but it can
be terribly frustrating. If you worship with a small, rural congregation, you may be loved and well fed, and you may be given free
rein with the youth group, but don't expect to make any changes
overnight—especially if they affect the budget. Other congregations are innovative and ministry-oriented, but may fall apart
when leadership changes. I have known several urban churches
which seemed to be ideal models of the New Testament church.
They cared about each member as a whole person, they min-

istered to the poor and the alienated, their worship was sponta-
neous and jubilant. But when a leadership crisis developed,
members scattered, feeling alone and betrayed.

Probably the characteristic of a congregation which first stands
out is its friendliness—or coldness—to newcomers. A friendly
church is usually interested in evangelism, or at least in gaining
new members. But don't write off a church that seems unfriendly
on the first visit—they may just be shy. Churches have self-images, just like individuals. The Lord may send you to a church
with a low self-image to encourage them. For instance, Ginny
started attending a small church in her neighborhood. She joined
a women's Bible class, but did not lead it. For a year or so she
simply got to know the women in the class. Most of them were
older and had children Ginny's age. They frequently invited her
over for dinner after church. In the meantime, Ginny shared herself, telling about her involvement with a children's Bible study
and her summer experience in Appalachia. Gradually, the women
began to realize that God could use them in ministry too. One
began volunteering at a home for mentally retarded children,
another went to church with her cleaning woman and discovered
a multitude of needs for food and clothing, which the class
adopted as an ongoing project.

When Ginny was transferred to another town, the class gave her
a Bible. In it the teacher wrote: "To Ginny, whose faithfulness to
our Lord is the greatest witness that our young men and women
are our hope. My prayer for you, Ginny, is that you will continue,
by His Spirit, the sweet fresh ministry you have shared with us
here." Ginny was stunned. She did not realize that she had a
ministry. She had merely loved the women in the class, and
allowed them to love her. That simple interaction had freed those
women from their low sense of self-worth and enabled them to
reach out to others.

To some extent, it is helpful if your own personality fits in with
the personality of a congregation. If you enjoy intergenerational

activities, you will probably want to look for a family-oriented church. Our present congregation scores high in this area. Children are a loved and welcome part of worship services, social events and educational experiences. No one complains when a child cries during the worship service or answers the pastor's rhetorical questions during the sermon. On the other hand, some churches have a highly structured program which carefully separates each age groups. Even the adult classes and activities are divided by age group. One church where I was a member started a new "young marrieds" Sunday-school class every five years, keeping the old ones intact. That enabled each class to focus on the needs and interests of a specific age group. There are advantages to each system. They appeal to different personalities.

Of course, you will want to find a church where there is *openness to sharing spiritually,* interest in Bible study and prayer, and a concern for the needs of others at home and abroad. Those seem like basic requirements when you begin your search. However, they are not always easily met. Even in strongly evangelical churches, you may find that no one, except for the pastor and elders, has ever prayed aloud in a group. Bible studies are more often taught than led. Sharing may be superficial and so clothed in lingo that it is more for appearances than for open communication. Missions interest can be stifled by denominational bureaucracy. But none of these apparent deficiencies should necessarily preclude God from calling us to such a church. He might want to use us there. He might also want to teach us something.

I spent a year in such a church. I'm not sure why I felt called to that church, but I did, and some very interesting things started to happen. First, the Lord met my own needs for fellowship by putting me in contact with a lively Roman Catholic Bible study and prayer group. That group was more excited about the Bible and applying it to their daily lives than any I have ever been part of. I grew tremendously through that experience. But something also happened in the church. The pastor changed from a mediocre preacher to an outstanding one. My life was changed through his preaching, too. Before moving to another state, I visited him to thank him for his sermons. I also mentioned that I had noticed a change in his preaching. He laughed. "Do you know why?" he asked. I shook my head. "I was preaching to you! Ever since I've been here, I've felt like no one cared what I preached. But I could tell you were listening, and you seemed to be right with me. So I would preach just for you. Thank you for revitalizing my ministry."

## Denominations and Independent Churches
Another consideration in choosing a church is *affiliation*—whether to stay within a denomination or to look for an independent church. For years I vacillated back and forth between the two. There is a trade-off with either one. Often the choice seems to be between stability and spontaneity.

Some of the most lively churches I have known were independent. They were not tied down to what was done in the past, because the congregation was usually very new. They were not accountable to denominational authorities, so were able to be innovative with programs and worship. They could use any hymnal they wanted. They could write their own Sunday-school material or disband Sunday school altogether. Members were enthusiastic and deeply committed.

But when a leadership crisis occurs in an independent church there is usually no higher authority to mediate differences. Personality clashes among leaders can become clothed in spiritual terms and be heartbreaking and vicious. When a church is formed around the charismatic personality of one person, it can quickly die when the leader leaves.

Although doctrinal purity is often the precipitating factor in forming an independent church, there is also greater opportunity for it to be lost when there is no official denominational statement of belief. One dynamic independent church where I worshiped decided to write its own creed. The pastor and elders, though committed Christians, had no seminary training or knowledge of church history. The creed they wrote sounded strangely gnostic. The congregation subsequently slipped more and more into a hierarchical authority structure. The wisdom of the person "over" you began to carry more weight than the Scriptures. As the pressure to "submit" got stronger, I went back to my stuffy denominational church.

But not all independent churches fall apart or drift into heresy. Some are quite stable and doctrinally sound. I believe that God uses independent churches as a corrective when denominations become too caught up in bureaucracy or when their spiritual ardor wanes. I have probably experienced the greatest spiritual growth—and the deepest heartaches—in independent churches.

On the other hand, I have grown to appreciate the denominational bureaucracy and realize that in many ways it safeguards Christian freedom and lends stability. The order of worship, which at times seems to lack spontaneity, provides a balance to the service and encourages full congregational participation. What at times comes across as apathy and resistance to change is often a maturity which understands that everything new is not necessarily good.

A church, whether denominational or independent, should have *ties with other Christians* at home and abroad. A healthy church is willing to give generously of time, talent and money to spread the gospel in the world. They are faithful in praying for missionaries and Christian nationals in other lands. One church where I worshiped went a step further. When missionaries they supported were celebrating special occasions, like the dedication of a new building or their first missions conference, the church would send a delegation to attend. Not only did it encourage the missionaries and the nationals, but missions interest and support in the church skyrocketed.

We need to be accountable to Christians in other countries to maintain a biblical perspective. We are all victims of our culture.

For instance, when an Australian Nurses Christian Fellowship staff worker visited us several years ago, she spent time with student groups, summer camps and several workshops. Before leaving she said to me, "Do you realize how much authority you Americans give to psychology? You even interpret the Bible according to psychology." She was right. We began to evaluate our use of psychology much more carefully and critically.

Another example sticks vividly in my mind. Our seminary community was having a Halloween party, so my husband and I invited our friends from Tanzania to go with us. When we arrived at their apartment afterward they gave us a firm scolding. "The missionaries always told us that we had to give up the pagan customs of our culture. We are shocked that the seminary would allow such overt pagan practices on campus!" We had never thought about the pagan roots of Halloween; it was just fun to dress up in silly costumes. But then we began to consider the meaning of all the witches, goblins, red devils and ghosts and suddenly realized why our friends were so upset.

While all of these factors are important in choosing a church, you will not find one which meets all your criteria. There are no perfect churches. Every church is made up of sinful human beings trying to be faithful. However, each of us needs the church in order to remain alive—and humble—in the faith.

## The Body and Your Vocation

Even the best churches may not be able to adequately help us integrate our faith with what we do on the job. For instance, Lisa, a new graduate nurse, suddenly found herself surrounded by dying people when she began working in a cancer hospital. Each time a patient died Lisa felt a surge of doubt, fear and uncertainty well up inside herself. Death was so ugly, so full of tubes, machines, bad odors and human tragedy. Somehow all she had learned about death in Sunday school and church seemed trite and unrealistic. Lisa needed to talk to somebody. She tried talking to several people at church and to her roommate, Jane, but it just seemed to make them feel uncomfortable. Jane, an English teacher with no personal experiences with death, finally told Lisa, "This is all so morbid, I wish you wouldn't unload it on me!"

Then a friend at work invited Lisa to a Nurses Christian Fellowship Bible study series on death. There she found a group of other Christian nurses who listened empathetically to her feelings of anger and despair. Many of them had experienced the same frustrations. She also discovered that the Bible offers a great deal more in the way of encouragement and support than she remembered. The group prayed for her and for the families of her patients who had died. She went back to work feeling loved, supported and hopeful.

Christian nurses, teachers, lawyers, physicians, social workers, business executives and numerous other special interest groups have formed fellowships to deal with the unique problems and opportunities in their fields (see appendix for names and addresses of some). A vocational fellowship group is not a substitute for the church; it is a supplement. It can help you to deal with the special concerns, pressures and ethical issues you confront daily in a way that the heterogeneous church community cannot. It can also be an effective setting for evangelism among your colleagues.

Another opportunity for fellowship and evangelism related to your job is in a Bible study over lunch at work. Some factory Bible studies include everyone from the president of the company to the assembly line workers. A hospital Bible study can include nurses, physicians, housekeeping personnel and kitchen workers. In fact, one hospital Bible study was a key factor in settling a union dispute because some of the leaders in both labor and management were in the group. They were able to tell the others on the negotiating teams, "We have prayed about this and come up with a compromise." The compromise was accepted.

God has called us to be his people. Every aspect of our life and work is related to our calling to be in Christ. To be in Christ is to be in the body of Christ—the fellowship of his people. Our life in the body equips us for ministry in our jobs, our communities and the world. Hebrews 10:23-25 exhorts us: "Let us hold fast the confession of our hope without wavering, for he who promised is faithful; and let us consider how to stir up one another to love and good works, not neglecting to meet together, as is the habit of some, but encouraging one another, and all the more as you see the Day drawing near."

# 7
# The Fruit
# of Our Labors

T HAT FIRST PAYCHECK— what a beautiful sight! Many of us have been tempted to frame it. It represents years of preparation and hours of hard work. A paycheck says in concrete terms, "You are so important that we will pay you for being here." Suddenly a whole new world opens up. You can make a down payment on a car, rent an apartment, travel. Money spells freedom and independence.

Then comes the first performance evaluation. The words keep ringing in your ears, "John shows strong potential as a leader. His abilities in problem solving are clearly demonstrated in his job performance." The affirmation makes you strive to do better and gives you a sense of self-worth. You know you can do the job. Your work situation helps you grow and mature.

Eventually the people you have known all your life begin to treat you with new respect. Your colleagues and those over whom you have authority seem to trust and admire you. You may have students looking up to you as their teacher or hospital patients entrusting you with their lives. You may be responsible for thousands of dollars. One way or another, work provides status.

Money, personal growth and status are the fruits of our labors. Although at times money will be scarce and a job will become a source of discouragement, for most college graduates in our society material possessions come easily and employment provides opportunity for growth and status. Jesus clearly taught that all fruits of our labor belong to God. He told a parable in Luke 12:16-21 describing the foolishness of a man who kept building bigger barns to store his riches, but did not consider his responsibilities before God.

## Money

Money is one of the primary fruits of our labors. To many people in our society it is the concrete measure of our worth as persons. In itself, money is a neutral or even good thing. It is important for meeting our personal needs and the needs of our families. But 1 Timothy 6:10 warns us: "The love of money is the root of all evils; it is through this craving that some have wandered away from the faith and pierced their hearts with many pangs."

Money and faith are closely related. The Lord has promised to meet our needs for food, clothing and shelter (Mt 6:25-33). He does not begrudge us the necessities of life; he cares for us as a loving Father. Probably one of the most difficult tests of our faith in God comes through a willingness to give up our faith in money. It goes against human nature. For instance, would you be willing to close out your savings account in order to pay the tuition of an international student whose country suddenly cut off his funding? Would you take a three-month unpaid leave from your job to go on a short-term missions project? Would you quit a high-paying job and go back to school to prepare for a new calling, knowing that you will make far less in your new endeav-

or? Would you tithe seventy-five per cent of your income? Money seems to buy security and control. It is hard to let go of it.

In comparison to the salaries my friends in other fields were earning, nursing was a low-paying job. I never went hungry, but I never felt like I had any money to spare. Then I began to consider joining Nurses Christian Fellowship staff. The salary for a beginning staff worker was exactly half what I was earning. I was convinced that no one could possibly subsist on such a meager wage, but I decided to test it out.

For six months I lived on half my salary and put the rest in the bank. The results amazed me. My basic lifestyle did not change. I could still easily afford to pay the rent, buy groceries and take care of all the essentials. But my shopping habits changed radically. I suddenly realized that I had been shopping for entertainment, buying items which appealed to me whether I needed them or not. My closet was full of fad clothing I never wore. The refrigerator overflowed with rotting, molding food because I didn't use leftovers.

As my savings accumulated, it occurred to me that putting half my paycheck in the bank was not much of a faith commitment. For the next three months I gave away half my income. To my surprise, it didn't hurt. In fact, I began to see God at work in my life in such a powerful way that I no longer had any doubts about joining NCF staff. What's more, I discovered how much fun it can be to give away money.

God does not expect us to be foolish with our money, but sometimes our idea of foolishness differs from his. In Malachi 3:10 he tells us: "Bring the full tithes into the storehouse, that there may be food in my house; and thereby put me to the test, says the LORD of hosts, if I will not open the windows of heaven for you and pour down for you an overflowing blessing." That is quite a challenge. But everyone I know who has put God to the test over money has found him more than faithful. He does not always work according to our plans, though.

Jackie believed God was calling her to go to Central America for a short-term missions experience. Although she had just enough money in her savings account to cover airfare and expenses, she was sure the Lord would provide gifts to cover the cost so she would not have to dip into her savings. "It would be such a witness to my non-Christian neighbors," she told me. However, the money did not come. Jackie went anyway, and the neighbors were deeply impressed with her willingness to sacrifice for God. They wanted to know more about this God who could inspire such faithfulness. When we are willing to take financial risks, the Lord works powerfully in us and through us. That is part of the "overflowing blessing" of Malachi 3:10.

The Lord also provides for our physical needs when we are free with our gifts and offerings. Part of the way he does that is through the generosity of other Christians. In 2 Corinthians 8:2 Paul describes the dire situation of the church in Macedonia, "In a severe test of affliction, their abundance of joy and their extreme poverty have overflowed in a wealth of liberality on their part." Even in their poverty they were eager to give beyond their means to help others in need. Paul then appeals to the Corinthian church to help the Macedonians. Although it might have been tempting to sit back and say, "Well, if the Macedonians were really doing God's will they wouldn't be poor," Paul didn't do that. He commended them for their generosity and instructed the Corinthians to do their part as well.

The Lord gives his gifts to individual members of the body to be used for the benefit of all. That includes financial gifts (Rom 12:8). When God richly blesses us financially, we have the responsibility to share with the body as a whole. Paul continues his exhortation in 2 Corinthians 9:6-7: "The point is this: he who sows sparingly will also reap sparingly, and he who sows bountifully will also reap bountifully. Each one must do as he has made up his mind, not reluctantly or under compulsion, for God loves a cheerful giver." We are partners with other Christians who need our financial support in order to minister.

Giving can be a joyous ministry. Paul continues: "He who supplies seed to the sower and bread for food will supply and multiply your resources and increase the harvest of your righteousness. You will be enriched in every way for great generosity, which through us will produce thanksgiving to God; for the rendering of this service not only supplies the wants of the saints but also overflows in many thanksgivings to God. Under the test of this service, you will glorify God by your obedience in acknowledging the gospel of Christ, and by the generosity of your contribution for them and for all others" (2 Cor 9:10-13). Perhaps that explains why giving can be so much fun. It is an expression of faith that God will continue to provide, as well as a commitment to fellow believers. We can relax and enjoy life because we know God is faithful. We can feel a sense of accomplishment because we know God is at work and will use our gifts to fulfill his purposes. We have a sense of love and relatedness with other Christians because we experience our interdependency firsthand.

Money is a fruit of our labors, but even though we worked for it, it is still a gift from God. We need to learn to hold onto it loosely and give of it freely. In order to give responsibly, it helps to have a plan. In our family, the first ten per cent goes to the local church. Then we pledge specific additional amounts toward the support of a number of missionaries, special projects and other ministries. Every year we sit down and review our financial situation, consider new needs and revise our commitments. Planned giving does not need to limit flexibility. We have been amazed at how, when needs arise, the money has been there to give. We have also stood in awe as God provided for our own needs in tight times.

Money and the things it buys can become our masters if we do not remember that they belong to the Lord. He has merely given us stewardship over them. We are free to enjoy what he has entrusted to us, but only as long as we do not hoard it. Matthew 6:24 tells us: "No one can serve two masters; for either he will hate the one and love the other, or he will be devoted to the one and despise the other. You cannot serve God and mammon." We must constantly be on guard that we do not allow money and material possessions to rule our lives or limit our commitment to Christ. Once we choose to serve Christ, our money must serve him as well.

But money is not the only fruit of our labors. For those called to homemaking or volunteer work, there may be no money involved at all. Perhaps one of the most satisfying results of work is the personal and professional growth we experience.

## Growth

Martha quit a nursing job to raise her family, but when the Nurses Christian Fellowship staff worker told her about the struggling group of students who wanted to start a Bible study at a nearby school of nursing, she decided she could help out. Martha was amazed at how eager the students were for her advice and support and how warmly they received her. As they worked together the group thrived. The following year they had five Bible studies on campus, and Martha began helping students in another school as well. Eventually they started having area-wide meetings, then all-day workshops and weekend retreats. Martha's confidence and competence increased as her work expanded.

Bill's personal and professional growth occurred in a secular job. He started his first job feeling incompetent and insecure, but by the time he had spent six years with the same company he had developed into a strong leader. He was then able to use those skills in developing an evangelism program for his church. His pastor had been feeling frustrated because no one seemed interested in evangelism, so Bill approached him with a plan for motivating and training a group of twelve people who would in turn train others. The plan worked.

Alicia also grew in a secular job. A university professor, she earned a reputation as an excellent teacher who truly cared for her students. She became concerned that nothing in the curriculum related to the spiritual dimension of persons, even though the school's philosophy stated that each person is a "biological-psychosocial-spiritual being." She presented a plan to the curriculum committee for integrating spirituality, from a Christian perspective, into the curriculum. The committee trusted Alicia and approved her proposal.

We are stewards just as much over our personal and professional abilities as over our finances. Ephesians 4:15-16 tells us: "We are to grow up in every way into him who is the head, into Christ, from whom the whole body, joined and knit together by every joint with which it is supplied, when each part is working properly, makes bodily growth and upbuilds itself in love." The growth we experience through work is not merely for our own satisfaction or for the benefit of our employers; it is also for building up the body of Christ.

Martha, Bill and Alicia demonstrated this ministry of stewardship over their abilities in three different ways, but each was faithful with the gifts God gave. Martha worked as a volunteer in a parachurch organization; Bill worked through the local church; and Alicia found her ministry within her job. Serving God does not necessarily mean doing something religious. It does mean helping people physically, emotionally and spiritually. This may include sharing the gospel message with a colleague, but it also encompasses working for justice in society, feeding the hungry and loving the unlovely.

For instance, Joe, a construction foreman, constantly criticized poor people. He believed that people were poor because they were lazy. Then one summer he took a month off during his peak season to go with a church mission project to build a clinic in Appalachia. The people in the mountain village pitched in to help with the building, cooked meals for the volunteers and housed them at night. When Joe realized that many of the people were going hungry in order to provide food for the workmen, he felt humbled and guilty. He saw how hard the people worked, and yet there were no paying jobs available. Joe switched from being a critic to being an advocate for the needs of the poor.

Mary Ann strongly opposed abortion. A nurse, she refused to work in labor and delivery because it would mean assisting with abortions. She self-righteously defended her stand, claiming that as a Christian she could not participate in evil. However, it took several years before she realized that her position required positive action as well as negative. Eventually she became involved in an organization that supports pregnant women physically, emotionally and spiritually so that they can carry their babies to term instead of aborting them.

Harry and Carol worked hard to help establish a Christian school so that their children could receive a good education with a biblical perspective. Then it occurred to them that the high tuition made it impossible for parents of low and moderate incomes to send their children to the school. They campaigned to have tuition based on ability to pay, even though it meant that they would pay double what some others paid.

## Status
Status is another by-product of work. Even the most inexperienced college graduate has status in the eyes of underclassmen, and everyone who works has respect and influence related to his or her occupation.

There is power in status. I am becoming increasingly aware of the importance of my status as a mother. Today I stood talking to a friend, leaning against a wall with my hands thrust into my back pockets. Janell stood right beside me, also leaning against the wall, her hands carefully placed in her back pockets. When I brush my teeth, she has to brush hers. If I prop my feet up on the coffee table, she sits on the edge of the sofa, struggling to reach the coffee table with her toes. She is also enthusiastic about praying. Every time we put her in her crib or into her highchair, she folds her hands and bows her head. Whenever she sees a Bible, she opens it on her lap and gets into prayer position. As Janell's mother, I have a powerful influence on her.

We are stewards of our status. The example we set may speak louder than any verbal presentation of the gospel. When people respect and admire us because of our behavior on the job, our verbal witness gains added strength. But status can be a misunderstood and misused tool in some contemporary evangelistic efforts.

The letter of James (2:1-9) contains strong warnings against honoring Christians for their wealth and status while discriminating against the poor and unpopular. The church was never intended to be a private club of beautiful people. Yet too often we hear the "gospel of success" instead of the gospel of the crucified Lord. Celebrities frequently appear in books and magazines, on television and the lecture circuit, proclaiming that God made them happy, healthy and successful. The implication is that accepting Jesus Christ guarantees a victorious and problem-free life. I'm not sure if Jesus or the apostle Paul or Peter or James would be invited on many talk shows today. Who wants to hear about all that suffering?

One celebrity made a profession of faith in Christ after having been an outspoken Black Muslim. Presently, his statements are so confusing that no one seems quite sure if he is a Christian, Muslim, Jew, Moonie or agnostic, but Christian groups are still using him as a speaker because of his status. We seem to defend our faith by saying, "See, we're okay, because so-and-so is one of us." That is a far cry from Jesus' attitude in Luke 6:26 when he said, "Woe to you, when all men speak well of you, for so their fathers did to the false prophets."

We are not to use status to communicate that being a Christian is glamorous or even socially acceptable. Nor can we tell people,

"If you become a Christian, you will be like me." To do so is to witness to human success, not to Christ.

Most of us are not celebrities, so we don't have to worry about other people emulating our faith to gain outstanding success. However, we still can use our status to manipulate others into faith on false pretenses. For example, when I was in college I knew a Christian professor who put Bible verses at the end of her exam papers. An ongoing rumor maintained that she would give you a higher grade if you cut the verses off and took them with you. Those who tried it insisted it worked. They further insisted that if you went to her to complain about your test grade and mentioned how much the verses meant to you, she would raise your grade. I don't know if there was any truth to my classmates' perception, but the effect was clearly manipulative.

We can manipulate people by somehow indicating to them that we will love them better or spend more time with them if they become Christians. When I was a campus staff worker, a student would sometimes come to me, claiming I had brought her to the Lord and ask me to disciple her. It was a tremendous boost to my ego. But occasionally I later found that I was being used because that student had "become a Christian" several times before in other campus Christian groups and had been discipled by their staff. It is important to discern whether people are being drawn to Christ or to our status.

Stewardship over our status means first giving it over to the Lord, realizing that he gave it to us for his purposes. I have a friend who exemplifies this kind of stewardship. In a high administrative position in a children's hospital, she has used her influence to facilitate development of a Sunday school for the children, to encourage nurses to form Bible study and prayer groups, and to establish a system which delivers top-quality health care with compassion. But she is also a servant. At a task-force meeting I was leading, she served refreshments and baby-sat for one of the participants. When introducing herself to the group she merely said, "I work at Children's Hospital." After three days together, the mother of the child being baby-sat asked, "Just what do you do at Children's Hospital?" After my friend replied, the mother looked at me and said, "Well, you certainly do provide qualified baby sitters!"

That is stewardship of status. Status is to be used when appropriate to accomplish God's purposes, but tucked away in a back pocket when it would only serve to alienate or intimidate. It is not an easy task. We can become overly impressed with our power or prestige on the job and expect family and friends to treat us with equal respect at home. We can become so accustomed to being served that we forget how to serve.

Yet we must not hesitate to use our status when necessary. Sometimes that may jeopardize our position. The "whistle-blower" who reports corruption in a company is often quickly replaced. The supervisor who will not tolerate illegal or unsafe practices by employees may end up in a lengthy lawsuit. Even the employee who merely does a good job when coworkers do not may be ostracized and ridiculed. Unless we constantly remember that our status belongs to God, we can too easily be tempted to protect it at the expense of honesty and justice.

The Lord gives Christians status to maintain order and establish justice in the world. He may also use it to enhance our testimony, but church history provides some interesting examples to the contrary. Jesus chose his disciples from among those with the least status in society. The apostle Paul lost his status with the Jewish community by becoming a Christian. As long as Christians were the persecuted underdogs, the faith spread with purity and fervor. Then, in the fourth century, the emperor Constantine declared Christianity an official religion and began marching captured armies through rivers to baptize them. As Christianity subsequently became the official religion of kings and others in power, it became lukewarm, corrupted and weak.

Before we become too enamored with power and status, we

would do well to remember that Satan used power to tempt Jesus in the wilderness. Jesus clearly named it what it was—a call to idolatry. Satan continues to tempt God's people with a similar form of idolatry. "If you will just overlook the illegal operations here, you will be promoted." "If you can get articles published in the right journals and pad your dossier with false praise—we don't care how you teach—you will receive tenure." "If you will work overtime seven days a week . . ." "If you will divorce your husband and marry your boss . . ." The only really important status is our status in God's kingdom. That frees us to answer with Jesus, "You shall worship the Lord your God, and him only shall you serve" (Lk 4:8).

However, status can be used to the glory of God. Responsible use of status may include modeling, influence and action. Modeling is an indirect form of influence. When a person who is admired and respected by others models a lifestyle of faith and morality while professing to be a Christian, the behavior is likely to be imitated. It helps a child to maintain Christian beliefs and behavior at school when the teacher is a Christian whose actions are consistent with his or her beliefs.

Influence requires a little more boldness. For instance, Bill worked for a city government agency which had a policy against using city-owned buildings for religious purposes. When employees began a lunch-time prayer group, they were informed that their meetings were illegal and would have to stop. Bill petitioned the city council to change the policy, using the First Amendment right to free exercise of religion as a basis. The city council respected Bill as a loyal administrator and agreed that his arguments had merit. They changed the policy.

Action is influence taken one step further. For instance, Carla was a nursing supervisor in an outpatient clinic of a large city hospital. Most of the patients were on welfare, and the clinic staff assumed they had nothing to do besides wait to be seen by a doctor. Therefore, they did not schedule appointments; they just told all the patients to come at one o'clock. The result was utter chaos in the clinic, with babies crying and restless children running around. The patients were usually so angry by the time they saw a doctor that they could not cooperate with the prescribed treatment. Carla decided it was time for action. She changed the system so that each patient received a specific appointment time, and she insisted that personnel adhere to the schedule as closely as possible. She also worked to get funding to make the waiting room facilities more pleasant, and to provide a playroom for the children and changing tables in the restrooms.

Money, growth, status—all are fruits of our labors, and all are gifts from God. Or perhaps it would be better to say that all are on loan to us from God. We can hang onto them tightly and use them only for our own selfish desires, but if we do we will lose them. Instead, Jesus calls us to invest them in his kingdom, to let him multiply their value by using them for his purposes. By doing so, we gain meaning and purpose in our lives and our work.

# 8
# Hearing
# God's Call

$\mathbf{M}$OST OF US secretly yearn for a spectacular call from God. We want to be sure that the choices we make are really God's will. When it came to joining Nurses Christian Fellowship staff, I was no exception. Although I thoroughly enjoyed working with NCF as a volunteer, I was not at all sure I wanted to make it a full-time job. The low pay, the need to raise support, the prospect of constant travel over unfamiliar territory and the necessity of leaving a secure job that I loved—all seemed overwhelming. When my staff worker asked me to consider NCF staff, I laughed and said, "The Lord would have to hit me over the head to convince me." But I did agree to pray with her about it. In fact, right then and there I propped my feet on the chair ahead of me and bowed my head to pray—striking my forehead on the back of the chair. A huge knot rose up on my forehead and stayed there for three days. That wasn't exactly what I had in mind, but I took it for a sign—for at least five minutes, when the pain subsided. Then I decided there must be a better way to be sure of God's call.

Where I ended up was back where I started in high school with my research approach to decision making. I began talking with other staff members to gain a fuller picture of what the job entailed, tried living on the pay I would receive as a staff member, became more involved as a volunteer and even did some traveling with a staff worker. In the meantime, I sought counsel from mature Christians who knew me well and established a prayer partnership with a friend who was also considering staff work. My quiet times became a constant dialog with God about the prospect of joining staff. I confessed my fears and reservations, and God reassured me through Scripture that he would be with me, equip me and guide me. When I finally decided to go on staff, it was with the firm conviction that the Lord wanted me there.

God communicates his will to us in a variety of ways. Signs and wonders are probably the least common and the least reliable. There is danger in overspiritualizing coincidences and unusual occurrences. Just because you receive a job offer on your birthday and the salary is exactly one thousand times your age does not mean God is calling you to that job. Or if, right after you pray for a husband, a man you have long admired calls and asks you for a date, he is not necessarily the husband you have been praying to find.

In general, God works through sanctified reason to guide us into his will. James 1:5 tells us, "If any of you lacks wisdom, let him ask God, who gives to all men generously and without reproaching, and it will be given him." James does not tell us that God will give us the exact answer, but that he will give us the wisdom to find it. He does that through prayer; Bible study; personal interests, desires and abilities; and the counsel of wise people. He has also given us an overview of his purposes in the world to guide us, as well as some clear moral guidelines.

We have spent a major portion of this book looking at God's

purposes for us in our vocation. We are here to live in relation-ship to God and to contribute to his ongoing work of creation and redemption. In some way, our work should be an expression of worship, a means of service and evangelism, and an exercise of stewardship. That encompasses a wide range of vocational choices. A plumber who cheerfully arrives at six o'clock in the morning to fix an overflowing drain, having had his prayer time in the truck on the way, is fulfilling God's qualifications. So is a business executive who manages a department with fairness and effectiveness in order to produce a needed product, while gently sharing his faith with coworkers.

Some jobs, of course, do not fit God's purposes—those that are clearly illegal or immoral, or ones which require dishonesty or deception. God does not call anyone to be a prostitute or a drug dealer or an embezzler. However, he does use even our past sins to his glory at times.

Surprisingly, many admirable and clearly Christian vocations may not fit into God's purposes for you. If you find yourself in a job you hate so much that you cannot consider it an expression of worship, you probably need to look elsewhere. For instance, Janice became a nurse because she wanted to please her father and because she thought all Christians should work in a field that directly serves the sick and the poor. However, she never got used to the routine. She always felt incompetent. Unexpected emergencies left her flustered and unable to function. She ago-nized over going to work each day. Nursing was probably not God's will for Janice.

Any job will present difficulties in adjustment at first. Janice was wise to struggle through a full year in her nursing job and then to try another type of nursing before finally deciding to become a secretary. The secretarial job was low pressured, predictable and a good outlet for Janice's perfectionism. She blossomed and thor-oughly enjoyed meeting the needs of only one person, her boss, rather than a hospital unit full of seriously ill people.

## Using Your Gifts

For some reason, many Christians think that God's will has to be the thing we least want to do. The opposite is actually the case. In Romans 12:6-8, we are told: "Having gifts that differ according to the grace given to us, let us use them: if prophecy, in proportion to our faith; if service, in our serving; he who teaches, in his teaching; he who exhorts, in his exhortation; he who contributes, in liberality; he who gives aid, with zeal; he who does acts of mercy, with cheerfulness." We usually enjoy doing the things we do well. It gives us personal satisfaction and often brings praise and encouragement from others. In this passage, Paul exhorts the Romans to major in those areas where God has gifted them. He does not say, "Well, you may be good at preaching, but why don't you try social work instead; it will keep you humble." The first step in discerning God's will for your life is to assess your gifts and interests. The Lord made you the way you are for a purpose, so it only makes sense to consider what he had in mind when he gave you a special personality and unique gifts. There are numerous ways to do this.

1. Take advantage of vocational counseling offered through schools and other agencies. You may be overlooking something which would suit you perfectly simply because you haven't heard of it. At one Urbana missionary convention a veterinarian with the peculiar specialty of camels, goats and llamas registered with InterCristo, a computer matching service for Christian mission organizations. When he received his print-out, he was amazed to find a mission board desperately in need of someone with exactly those qualifications.

2. Make a list of the activities you really enjoy. For instance, you might list participating in sports, reading, leading small groups, talking with people, being with teen-agers, traveling. Then try to think of as many vocations as possible where you could use those interests. Using the list above you might consider the following: professional athlete, high-school coach, youth pas-

tor, camp director, social worker, teacher, sports physician, and any number of other creative ideas. Ask a friend to help you brainstorm.

3. Test out the vocations you are considering. Try a temporary or part-time job in a field that interests you, or volunteer to assist a person who does the work you are considering. I learned I enjoyed staff work by doing it as a volunteer and traveling briefly with a staff member. At another time, I learned I disliked being a librarian (even though I love books) by working part-time in a library one summer.

4. Seek the counsel of mature Christians, teachers and friends who know you well, and talk to people who are working in your area of interest. Try to determine whether your skills and interests match the job requirements. A young woman came to me recently because she was thinking about going to nursing school. Although she was a qualified computer programmer and held a responsible position, she was restless because she wanted to be more involved with people, especially children. Instead of steering her toward nursing, I brainstormed with her about how she could use her present skills (which she enjoyed using), but combine them with more interaction with people. She ended up working as a computer consultant for the school system, helping children write computer programs. She also started presenting children's sermons once a month during church services.

Once you have assessed your interests and gifts and matched them with a few possibilities, you should have at least some leads for further exploration. Now it is time to narrow down the options and make a tentative decision. I say "tentative" because no career decision is irrevocable. You can change your mind and your major while in college. You can graduate to find your field of interest has no job openings. Or, you can work in a field for several years and then switch to another career. You may even get fired. But you have to aim somewhere if you want to move ahead, and that requires a decision.

## Making a Decision

In the decision-making process, the place to start is with prayer. That is more than just pleading, "Lord, show me your will." It is important to meditate and to listen. Talk to the Lord about what you really want in a vocation. Confess your weaknesses and fears. One concern I confessed to the Lord when I was considering joining NCF staff was that I did not believe I was an evangelist. He answered in an amazing way. That very day, the phone rang. A professor from the university called to say, "A student of mine gave me a New Testament, and I've read Matthew, Mark and Luke. Jesus intrigues me; I'd like to know more about him. This student said you could tell me more." Once I recovered from shock, I told her to read John and meet with me the next day. She became a Christian; I filled out my staff application.

Another way that God speaks to us is through the Scriptures. The Bible is not a fortune cookie. It should not be used in a magical way. I have a friend who used to plan her day by opening the Bible at random and pointing to a verse. She wound up doing some very strange things until a wise pastor firmly told her, "You are using your Bible like a lottery box!" God communicates to us through the Scriptures by revealing his character and his general will for us. For instance, throughout the Bible we can see deep concern for the poor and oppressed. We see a focus on eternal values rather than material gain. There are repeated themes of love for others, justice in society, mercy in human relationships. We also see God's chosen people involved in mundane occupations like carpentry, shepherding, fishing, tentmaking and tax collecting. Looking more closely at those people, we see that they were not vocationally limited by what they did on the job. Jesus was a carpenter, David a shepherd, Peter a fisherman, Paul a tentmaker, and Matthew a tax collector.

The Lord speaks through the Scriptures to remind us that he will be with us and equip us to do the jobs he calls us to do. I lived in the Psalms for six months while trying to decide whether to join NCF staff. I could identify strongly with the psalmists' doubts, fears and frustrations. But I also felt reassured by the clear focus on God's faithfulness in the midst of turmoil. The Epistles gave me a good picture of God's priorities and helped me see that many of my objections were merely lack of faith. A prayerful reading of Scripture can become an intimate conversation with God.

Once you sense God's general direction for your life and have a possible career or two in mind, you are ready to collect data on potential jobs. Look into practical considerations like salary, benefits, opportunities for advancement, hours and scheduling (will it require weekend work? evenings? overtime?). Determine whether you can be yourself or if you will be expected to play status games. Will you be free to share your faith? Does the job offer equal opportunity for men, women and minorities—or can your being there bring change? Do others in that job setting seem satisfied, or is there a rapid turnover in personnel? How secure is the position?

No job is perfect. You will have to weigh the pros and cons prayerfully before coming to a decision. For instance, when Jerry graduated with a B.S. in math and computer science, he was offered both a teaching job in a local high school and a position in an industry fifty miles away. The teaching job matched his skills and interests and was close to his fiancée's place of employment. The industrial job paid a much higher salary, the benefits were excellent, and opportunities for advancement abounded. However, the job required a great deal of travel and overtime, and the personnel director told Jerry that the company expected their executives to live in certain neighborhoods, drive late-model cars and wear appropriately tailored suits. Jerry and his fiancée, Diane, prayed over the information on each job.

In considering the industrial job, they asked God if he was giving them the gift of giving. With a high salary, they would be able to generously support their church and quite a few missionaries. But they would also be expected to spend much more than they wanted for a house, a car and clothing. Diane felt that her own calling might be squelched in that setting. She would have to look for a new job and would also be expected to entertain Jerry's colleagues frequently. Both Jerry and Diane felt uncomfortable about accepting the job offer after they had prayed over and discussed all the details.

The teaching job also had drawbacks. The salary was so low that Diane would have to continue working even after children were born. Opportunities for advancement were extremely limited. However, Jerry had a gift for working with youth. He enjoyed being with teen-agers and delighted in helping them learn. As a youth-group adviser during his college days, he found himself being a role model and confidant for many teens who wanted to grow in their faith. Jerry accepted the teaching job and considered it a call from God.

Being sure of your calling will help you over the rough times of a new job. Almost any job has its drawbacks. Unless Jerry believed he was called to teaching, he might have felt strongly tempted to switch to the higher-paying industrial job when the principal began making unrealistic demands and the union called a strike and his students were disrespectful and unmotivated. Instead, he stuck with it, lived through the strike, won the confidence of the principal and earned the attention and respect of his students. That took ten years.

## Being Sure of Your Calling

A difficult adjustment period in your job does not necessarily indicate that you have made the wrong choice. For each of us there is a period of adjusting to routines, adapting to the personality quirks of our colleagues and supervisors, and learning from those with more experience. Being sure of your calling is something like the process of becoming Real described in the children's story *The Velveteen Rabbit*. The Rabbit was a newcomer to the nursery, trying to become oriented to his surroundings. He felt "very insignificant and commonplace." At one point, he asked the Skin Horse (the only other toy which was kind to him), "What is REAL? . . . Does it mean having things that buzz inside you and a stick-out handle?"

The Skin Horse replied, "REAL isn't how you are made. . . . It's a thing that happens to you. . . . It doesn't happen all at once. . . . You become. It takes a long time. That's why it doesn't often happen to people who break easily, or have sharp edges, or who have to be carefully kept. Generally, by the time you are REAL, most of your hair has been loved off, and your eyes drop out and you get loose in the joints and very shabby. But these things don't matter at all, because once you are REAL you can't be ugly, except to people who don't understand."[8]

The Skin Horse's wisdom was well spoken. All too often, a new college graduate comes roaring into a first job, buzzing inside and wielding a stick-out handle (called a degree). For four or more years he has been told how brilliant he is, how up-to-date his knowledge is, and how backward those people are in the world outside academe.

When I started my first nursing job, I was appalled at the way things were done. Many procedures and policies would have been considered outdated and improper by my instructors. I also met a strong prejudice against new graduates, especially baccalaureate graduates. While I mentally plotted a reform campaign, I found myself safely tucked away on the night shift with a motherly practical nurse who gently took me under her wing and made me REAL. She helped me see that many routines I questioned worked much better than the new approaches I had been taught. I learned to ask questions and to respect the experience of those who had been in nursing longer. Without Janie, my "Skin Horse," I probably would have alienated myself from my colleagues and accomplished very little.

It is important to give a job a fair chance. Unless you have walked into an absolutely unworkable disaster, a year's trial is probably a minimum. Some jobs which involve working with people in a long-term relationship may require a five-year trial period. For instance, almost every NCF staff worker feels like quitting at the end of the first year because not enough time has passed to see significant results of her ministry.

How can we be sure we are in the place God wants us to be? When it comes to our vocation, we may never be absolutely sure—especially if we rely on feelings as an indicator. Many pastors feel like leaving the ministry every Saturday night, but have great vision and hope on Monday morning. I often questioned my commitment to nursing when my alarm went off at 5:00 A.M., but usually felt good about it by 6:45. But there are indicators that can reinforce our sense of calling or help redirect us if necessary.

One very practical indicator is your supervisor's evaluation of your work. Most jobs provide you with periodic performance evaluations. If yours are generally good, then you are probably using your gifts and abilities effectively.

Writing personal and professional goals and reviewing them at least annually will help you see whether a job is meeting your original expectations. It will also help you evaluate how your job fits into your total vocation. If you find your job so consuming that you are unable to meet your personal goals, you might want to consider a change. For instance, if one of your goals was to meet weekly with a prayer group, but you have had to work overtime during all but three of the meetings this year, your life may be getting off balance.

A prayer partner or a group of Christians in your profession may help you maintain perspective. Sometimes the frustrations and discouragements you are experiencing with your job are common and only temporary. When you get together with other Christians and discover that they are facing similar problems, you can pray together about the situations and encourage one another. If necessary, you can work together to bring about change.

Periodically reviewing your job skills and growing competence may reinforce your call to your present work or nudge you to move on. It will highlight areas where you are most effective and may more clearly define your calling in a broader sense.

## Called to a Christian Setting

Christians are called to be "salt" and "light" in the everyday world (Mt 5:13-14), so in most cases the context of your calling will be secular. But sometimes the Holy Spirit calls Christians into church and parachurch vocations in order to provide effective leadership in the Christian community. Responding to such a calling is seldom easy. It may require sacrifices in salary, job security and status in the secular world. How can you be sure God is calling you into "full-time Christian service"? No pat formula exists, but here are some important guidelines.

There are a number of *wrong reasons* for considering full-time ministry in a Christian setting. If you find you are being pulled by any of the following motivations, the call is probably not from God. First, it is wrong to look for a "safe" Christian environment. No job is free from conflict, and dissension among Christians can be the most painful. Sometimes Christians can have much more unrealistic expectations of other Christians than non-Christians hold for us. Besides, the purpose of Christian ministry includes evangelism. If you have difficulty sharing your faith and values with non-Christians in a secular setting, it will become next to impossible once you begin spending most of your waking hours with other Christians.

Second, a sense of failure or dissatisfaction in your present job is not a reason to look for full-time Christian work. One of the major qualifications we look for in potential NCF staff is that they feel confident and competent in their present jobs. If you run away from current problems by joining a Christian organization or going to the mission field or becoming a pastor, you will most likely take your problems with you.

Third, don't look for Christian work because you want approval from others—parents, teachers, friends. You must make your own decision based on what you personally believe God is calling you to do. Persons who are easily swayed by others' expectations quickly break under the pressure of the ministry. Christian leaders are always vulnerable to unjust criticism, unrealistic expectations and strong disagreement.

Finally, you should not look for Christian work because you feel guilty. To some extent, we should feel guilty about the unmet physical, spiritual and emotional needs of others, especially when we are living in relative luxury. Real guilt should convict us to do all we can to help. But that is different from guilt feelings as a motivating factor. Pathological guilt feelings lead us to take personal responsibility for what should be a concern of the total body of Christ. It often makes us ungrateful for God's gifts and results in a self-righteous denial of what he intended us to be and do. For instance, Becky felt so guilty about the problems of the poor in India that she applied to a mission board. They rejected her, saying she did not have the appropriate skills and education. She decided to use her savings to pay her way and go to India on her own. Once she arrived, she volunteered to help wherever she could, but soon became overwhelmed with the vastness of the task and her inability to do anything about it. She came home when her tourist visa expired, feeling broken and discouraged.

Once you are sure that you are not feeling pushed into a Christian vocation by any of the above motives, you can evaluate whether God is truly leading you to work in a Christian setting. Just as he usually uses common, rational means to lead us into secular employment, so he does with a call to ministry. Here are some *good reasons* for full-time Christian work.

First, you may discover that God is using you in a particular ministry. You may begin working as a volunteer at church or with a parachurch organization, or you may go on a short-term missions project. Through this ministry you might find you can use many more of your gifts than you ordinarily do in your job. You may discover that your involvement becomes so time and energy consuming that you have to choose between your job and your ministry or risk burning out. Often, it just seems like the logical next move to go into full-time ministry.

Second, perhaps a need exists which you are especially well equipped to meet. This should not be considered a specific call unless it is coupled with other considerations. For instance, just because a mission station in Ghana is looking for an editor and you are one, you don't need to feel compelled to rush off to Ghana. But if you also find that you enjoy working with internationals, that you have a gift for evangelism and that you are able to adapt easily to other cultures, then maybe God is calling you to Ghana. If you are accepted by a mission board and arrive on Ghanaian soil, he most certainly is.

Third, maybe you have a special concern and a desire to get involved. Sometimes the Lord places certain interests in our hearts and minds. For example, Sharon became increasingly concerned about all the abortions being performed at a hospital where she was a nurse. So many of the women seemed totally uninformed about the alternatives to abortion and looked at it as merely a form of birth control. Sharon was also concerned about the attitudes of many Christians who were speaking out against abortion but doing nothing to help the pregnant women who were seeking abortions. Sharon finally concluded that, in order to be consistent with her beliefs, she had to join the staff of a Christian pregnancy counseling and support center.

Finally, God may be calling you into full-time ministry if you are successful in your present job. That may seem contradictory; however, one of the greatest needs in the Christian community is for experienced, competent leaders. Often the success a person finds in the secular world is excellent preparation for work in a Christian setting. For instance, John was in charge of obtaining foundation grants for a large university. He was also on the finance committee of a campus Christian organization. When he saw the difficulty staff constantly faced in raising financial support, he began looking for ways to obtain foundation grants. Eventually he decided that he could use his skills more fully by working for the organization full-time. Another example is Marian, a successful executive in a secular firm, who began to realize that a Christian organization she supported was on the verge of collapse for lack of a skilled administrator. She left her well-paying secular job to become business manager for the organization, knowing she would have to raise her own support as well as bring the organization up from financial disaster.

## Doing God's Will

Whether God calls you to work in a Christian setting or in a secular field, you are still in full-time Christian service. Probably the biggest key to deciding the context of your calling is to consider where God can use you most effectively. That does not necessarily have to be an either-or situation. You may work in a secular field, but also use your talents in a volunteer capacity in the church or a Christian organization. You may work for a Christian employer, but still deeply influence the secular world.

Most of us are "five talent" people (Mt 25:15). Jesus warns us, "Every one to whom much is given, of him will much be required" (Lk 12:48). We cannot sit back and savor the fruits of our labors as if they were personal possessions. We are required to use our talents for the benefit of the whole body and to meet the needs of our neighbors.

What has God called you to do? First of all, he has called you to be faithful to him. Then he calls each of us to be stewards of all he has entrusted to us. The key to doing God's will with our lives is to know God and to know ourselves, and then to put the two together. Once you have done that, you can trust God to accomplish his will in you. As Paul says in 1 Thessalonians 5:24, "He who calls you is faithful, and he will do it."

# Appendix

The following are groups of Christian academic and professional people who are thinking, writing and working on the relationship between the Christian view of things and their field.

### Literature

*The Conference on Christianity and Literature* welcomes student membership. It provides a quarterly journal called *Christianity and Literature* and regular conferences for discussion of key issues for lit majors and teachers. Write Conference on Christianity and Literature, c/o Professor Roy Battenhouse, President, English Department, Indiana University, Bloomington, IN 47401.

### Science

One of the strongest Christian societies of academic people is the American Scientific Affiliation. The ASA puts out a quarterly journal and bimonthly newsletter and holds regional and national meetings. Contact the ASA at American Scientific Affiliation, P.O. Box J, Ipswich, MA 01938.

### History

Since 1967 the *Conference on Faith and History* has brought together history majors, professional historians and others "who have an orientation toward historical concerns." A journal is published twice a year, and two meetings take place annually to discuss Christianity and history. Write to the Conference on Faith and History, Professor Richard Pierard, Secretary, Department of History,

Indiana State University, Terre Haute, IN 47809.

## Behavioral Sciences

Among the members of the *Christian Association for Psychological Studies* (CAPS) are "men and women engaged professionally in the fields of psychology, psychiatry, and related areas, such as physicians, nurses, ministers, social workers, sociologists, educators, chaplains, guidance counselors, and rehabilitation workers." A quarterly newsletter, annual convention and published proceedings of the convention are included in the membership privileges. Write to Christian Assoc. for Psychological Studies, The University Hills Christian Center, 2700 Farmington Rd., Farmington Hills, MI 48018.

Psychology students should also be aware of the *Journal of Psychology and Theology* published by the Rosemead Graduate School of Professional Psychology, 13800 Biola Ave., La Mirada, CA 90639.

## Social Work

The *National Association of Christians in Social Work* (NACSW) draws together working and studying social workers to probe the Christian perspective. An annual convention, a bimonthly newsletter, a journal and other publications come with membership. Contact the Nat'l Assoc. of Christians in Social Work, P.O. Box 90, St. Davids, PA 19087.

## Medical Fields

Nursing students should be aware of the *Nurses Christian Fellowship,* an official part of Inter-Varsity Christian Fellowship, which has staff and student groups in nursing schools all over the country. NCF has developed training programs for students and practicing nurses as well as Bible studies and a quarterly journal. Write to Nurses Christian Fellowship, 233 Langdon Street, Madison, WI 53703 for information about NCF and about the *Journal of Christian Nursing.*

The *Christian Medical Society* includes doctors and medical and dental students among its members. A quarterly journal, chapters at medical schools and overseas missionary projects are the major activities of the CMS. Write Christian Medical Society, P.O. Box 689, Richardson, TX 75080.

The *Christian Dental Society* can be contacted at 5235 Sky Trail, Littleton, CO 80123. Dentists with a concern for missions can also contact *Missionary Dentists,* in care of The Missionary Dentist, Inc., P.O. Box 7002, Seattle, WA 98133.

## Humanities

In addition to the journals and societies mentioned above, a general publication appealing primarily to Christian upperclassmen, graduate students and faculty is the *Christian Scholar's Review*, Bethel College, 3900 Bethel Dr., St. Paul, MN 55112.

## Law

The *Christian Legal Society* (P.O. Box 2069, Oak Park, IL 60303) and the *Lawyers' Christian Fellowship* (3931 E. Main Street, Columbus, OH 43213) are two societies that should be checked out by law students or pre-law undergrads. The CLS has a defined evangelical doctrinal statement. The main objective of the LCF is to carry out the Great Commission.

## Education

Education majors should investigate *National Educators Fellowship*, a rather conservative professional organization for Christians in public education. Write National Educators Fellowship, Inc., E. A. Patchen, Executive Secretary, 1410 W. Colorado Blvd., Pasadena, CA 91105.

## Sundry for Graduate Students and Others

Graduate students might find the *Christian Graduate* worth importing from England. It is a quarterly published by the Universities and Colleges Christian Fellowship. Broad topics of Christian interest are taken up in depth. Write *Christian Graduate*, 38 De Montfort Street, Leicester LE1 7GP, England.

Graduate students associated with Inter-Varsity have published *Crux*, a quarterly of advanced general interest related to topics in the humanities. Their address is 2130 Wesbrook Mall, Vancouver, B.C. V6T 1W6, Canada.

Waymeet, a Christian study center, has facilities including books, periodicals, tapes and a regular bulletin, called *Signposts*. Contact them at 229 College Street, Toronto, Ontario M5T 1R4, Canada.

# Notes

[1]Derek Kidner, *Genesis* (Downers Grove, Ill.: InterVarsity Press, 1967), p. 71.

[2]Brother Lawrence, *The Practice of the Presence of God* (Old Tappan, N.J.: Fleming H. Revell, 1958), p. 8.

[3]J. D. Douglas, ed., *The Illustrated Bible Dictionary,* Vol. 3 (Wheaton, Ill.: Tyndale, 1980), p. 1656.

[4]T. A. Kantonen, *A Theology for Christian Stewardship* (Philadelphia: Fortress Press, 1956), p. 100 ·

[5]See Ronald J. Sider, *Rich Christians in an Age of Hunger,* Rev. ed. (Downers Grove, Ill.: InterVarsity Press, 1984), pp. 15-49.

[6]J. D. Douglas, ed., *The New Bible Dictionary* (Grand Rapids, Mich.: Eerdmans, 1962), p. 676.

[7]See Charles Hummel, *The Tyranny of the Urgent* (Downers Grove, Ill.: InterVarsity Press, 1967).

[8]Margery Williams, *The Velveteen Rabbit* (New York: Doubleday, n.d.), pp. 16-17.

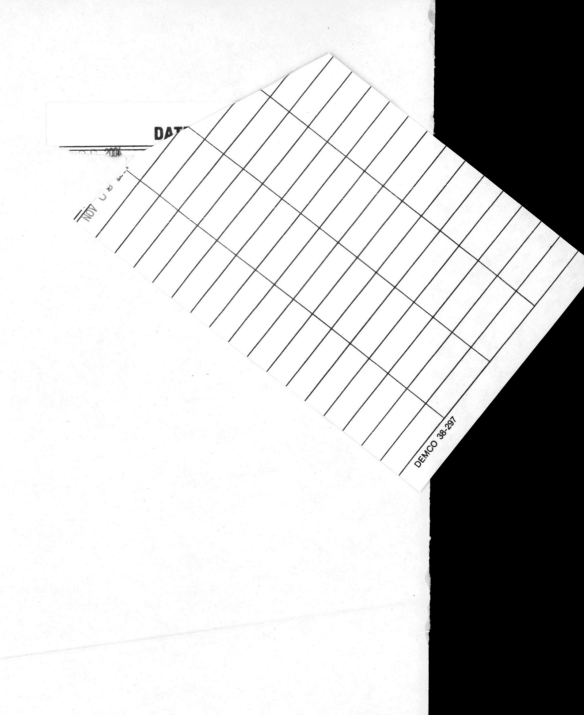